The IDG Books 60 Minute Guide S

We at IDG Books Worldwide created the *60 Minute Guide to CGI Programming with Perl 5* to meet your growing need for quick access to the most complete and accurate computer information available. Our books work the way you do: They focus on accomplishing specific tasks — not learning random functions. Our books are not long-winded manuals or dry reference tomes. In each book, expert authors tell you exactly what you can do with your new technology and software and how to evaluate its usefulness for your needs. Easy to follow, step-by-step instructions; comprehensive coverage; and convenient access in language and design — it's all here.

The authors of IDG books are uniquely qualified to give you expert advice as well as to provide insightful tips and techniques not found anywhere else. Our authors maintain close contact with end users through feedback from articles, training sessions, e-mail exchanges, user group participation, and consulting work. Because our authors know the realities of daily computer use and are directly tied to the reader, our books have a strategic advantage.

Our authors have the experience to approach a topic in the most efficient manner, and we know that you, the reader, will benefit from a "one-on-one" relationship with the author. Our research shows that readers make computer book purchases because they want expert advice. Because readers want to benefit from the author's experience, the author's voice is always present in an IDG book.

You will find what you need in this book whether you read it from cover to cover, section by section, or simply one topic at a time. As a computer user, you deserve a comprehensive resource of answers. We at IDG Books Worldwide are proud to deliver that resource with the *60 Minute Guide to CGI Programming with Perl 5*.

Brenda McLaughlin
Senior Vice President and Group Publisher
YouTellUs@idgbooks.com

60 Minute Guide to CGI Programming with Perl 5

Robert Farrell

IDG Books Worldwide, Inc.
Foster City, CA • Chicago, IL • Indianapolis, IN • Southlake, TX

60 Minute Guide to CGI Programming with Perl 5

Published by
IDG Books Worldwide, Inc.
An International Data Group Company
919 E. Hillsdale Blvd.
Suite 400
Foster City, CA 94404

Library of Congress Catalog Card No.: 95-81545

ISBN: 1-56884-780-7

Printed in the United States of America

10 9 8 7 6 5 4 3 2 1

1B/SR/QW/ZW/IN

Distributed in the United States by IDG Books Worldwide, Inc.

Distributed by Macmillan Canada for Canada; by Contemporanea de Ediciones for Venezuela; by Distribuidora Cuspide for Argentina; by CITEC for Brazil; by Ediciones ZETA S.C.R. Ltda. for Peru; by Editorial Limusa SA for Mexico; by Transworld Publishers Limited in the United Kingdom and Europe; by Academic Bookshop for Egypt; by Levant Distributors S.A.R.L. for Lebanon; by Al Jassim for Saudi Arabia; by Simron Pty. Ltd. for South Africa; by Pustak Mahal for India; by The Computer Bookshop for India; by Toppan Company Ltd. for Japan; by Addison Wesley Publishing Company for Korea; by Longman Singapore Publishers Ltd. for Singapore, Malaysia, Thailand, and Indonesia; by Unalis Corporation for Taiwan; by WS Computer Publishing Company, Inc. for the Philippines; by WoodsLane Pty. Ltd. for Australia; by WoodsLane Enterprises Ltd. for New Zealand. Authorized Sales Agent: Anthony Rudkin Associates for the Middle East and North Africa.

For information on where to purchase IDG Books Worldwide's books outside the U.S., contact IDG Books Worldwide's International Sales department at 415-655-3078 or fax 415-655-3281.

For information on foreign language translations, contact IDG Books Worldwide's Foreign & Subsidiary Rights department at 415-655-3018 or fax 415-655-3281.

For sales inquiries and special prices for bulk quantities, contact IDG Books Worldwide's Sales department at 415-655-3200 or write to the address above.

For information on using IDG Books Worldwide's books in the classroom or for ordering examination copies, contact IDG Books Worldwide's Educational Sales department at 800-434-2086 or fax 817-251-8174.

 is a trademark under exclusive license to IDG Books Worldwide, Inc., from International Data Group, Inc.

About the Author

Robert Farrell is a Research Scientist at Bellcore, a major telecommunications software and consulting company. He is the author of numerous publications in the areas of artificial intelligence, programming languages, and learning systems. He was part of the team that created www.bellcore.com. Mr. Farrell lives with his wife and son in Clinton, New Jersey.

Dedication

For Shari and Matthew

ABOUT IDG BOOKS WORLDWIDE

Welcome to the world of IDG Books Worldwide.

IDG Books Worldwide, Inc., is a subsidiary of International Data Group, the world's largest publisher of computer-related information and the leading global provider of information services on information technology. IDG was founded more than 25 years ago and now employs more than 7,700 people worldwide. IDG publishes more than 250 computer publications in 67 countries (see listing below). More than 70 million people read one or more IDG publications each month.

Launched in 1990, IDG Books Worldwide is today the #1 publisher of best-selling computer books in the United States. We are proud to have received 8 awards from the Computer Press Association in recognition of editorial excellence and three from Computer Currents' First Annual Readers' Choice Awards, and our best-selling ...*For Dummies*® series has more than 19 million copies in print with translations in 28 languages. IDG Books Worldwide, through a joint venture with IDG's Hi-Tech Beijing, became the first U.S. publisher to publish a computer book in the People's Republic of China. In record time, IDG Books Worldwide has become the first choice for millions of readers around the world who want to learn how to better manage their businesses.

Our mission is simple: Every one of our books is designed to bring extra value and skill-building instructions to the reader. Our books are written by experts who understand and care about our readers. The knowledge base of our editorial staff comes from years of experience in publishing, education, and journalism — experience which we use to produce books for the '90s. In short, we care about books, so we attract the best people. We devote special attention to details such as audience, interior design, use of icons, and illustrations. And because we use an efficient process of authoring, editing, and desktop publishing our books electronically, we can spend more time ensuring superior content and spend less time on the technicalities of making books.

You can count on our commitment to deliver high-quality books at competitive prices on topics you want to read about. At IDG Books Worldwide, we continue in the IDG tradition of delivering quality for more than 25 years. You'll find no better book on a subject than one from IDG Books Worldwide.

John J. Kilcullen

John Kilcullen
President and CEO
IDG Books Worldwide, Inc.

IDG Books Worldwide, Inc., is a subsidiary of International Data Group, the world's largest publisher of computer-related information and the leading global provider of information services on information technology. International Data Group publishes over 250 computer publications in 67 countries. Seventy million people read one or more International Data Group publications each month. International Data Group's publications include: **ARGENTINA:** Computerworld Argentina, GamePro, Infoworld, PC World Argentina; **AUSTRALIA:** Australian Macworld, Client/Server Journal, Computer Living, Computerworld, Digital News, Network World, PC World, Publishing Essentials, Reseller; **AUSTRIA:** Computerwelt, PC TEST; **BELARUS:** PC World Belarus; **BELGIUM:** Data News; **BRAZIL:** Annuário de Informática, Computerworld Brazil, Connections, Super Game Power, Macworld, PC World Brazil, Publish Brazil, SUPERGAME; **BULGARIA:** Computerworld Bulgaria, Networkworld/Bulgaria, PC & MacWorld Bulgaria; **CANADA:** CIO Canada, ComputerWorld Canada, InfoCanada, Network World Canada, Reseller World; **CHILE:** Computerworld Chile, GamePro, PC World Chile; **COLUMBIA:** Computerworld Colombia, GamePro, PC World Colombia; **COSTA RICA:** PC World Costa Rica/Nicaragua; **THE CZECH AND SLOVAK REPUBLICS:** Computerworld Czechoslovakia, Elektronika Czechoslovakia, PC World Czechoslovakia; **DENMARK:** Communications World, Computerworld Danmark, Macworld Danmark, PC World Danmark, PC World Danmark Supplements, TECH World; **DOMINICAN REPUBLIC:** PC World Republica Dominicana; **ECUADOR:** PC World Ecuador, GamePro; **EGYPT:** Computerworld Middle East, PC World Middle East; **EL SALVADOR:** PC World Centro America; **FINLAND:** MikroPC, Tietoverkko, Tietoviikko; **FRANCE:** Distributique, Golden, Info PC, Le Guide du Monde Informatique, Le Monde Informatique, Reseaux & Telecoms; **GERMANY:** Computer Business, Computerwoche, Computerwoche Extra, Computerwoche Focus, Electronic Entertainment, GamePro, I/M Information Management, Macwelt, PC Welt; **GREECE:** GamePro, Macworld & Publish; **GUATEMALA:** PC World Centro America; **HONDURAS:** PC World Centro America; **HONG KONG:** Computerworld Hong Kong, PCWorld Hong Kong, Publish in Asia; **HUNGARY:** ABCD CD-ROM, Computerworld Szamitastechnika, PC & Mac World Hungary, PC-X Magazine; **INDIA:** Computerworld India, PC World India, Publish in Asia; **INDONESIA:** InfoKomputer PC World, Komputek Computerworld, Publish in Asia; **IRELAND:** ComputerScope, PC Live!; **ISRAEL:** PC World 32 BIT, People & Computers; **ITALY:** Computerworld Italia, Computerworld Italia Special Editions, Lotus Italia, Macworld Italia, Networking Italia, PC Shopping, PC World Italia, PC World/Walt Disney; **JAPAN:** Macworld Japan, Nikkei Personal Computing, SunWorld Japan, Windows World Japan; **KENYA:** East African Computer News; **KOREA:** Hi-Tech Information/Computerworld, Macworld Korea, PC World Korea; **MACEDONIA:** PC World Macedonia; **MALAYSIA:** Computerworld Malaysia, PC World Malaysia, Publish in Asia; **MEXICO:** Computerworld Mexico, GamePro, Macworld, PC World Mexico; **MYANMAR:** PC World Myanmar; **NETHERLANDS:** Computable, Computer! Totaal, LAN Magazine, Macworld, Net Magazine; **NEW ZEALAND:** Computer Buyer, Computerworld New Zealand, MTB, Network World, PC World New Zealand; **NICARAGUA:** PC World Costa Rica/Nicaragua; **NIGERIA:** PC World Africa; **NORWAY:** Computerworld Norge, Computerworld Privat, CW Rapport Klient/Tjener, CW Rapport Nettverk & Telecom, CW Rapport Offentlig Sektor, IDG's KURSGUIDE, Macworld Norge, Multimedia World, PC World Ekspress, PC World Nettverk, PC World Norge, PC World's Produktguide, Windows World; **PAKISTAN:** Computerworld Pakistan, PC World Pakistan; **PANAMA:** GamePro, PC World Panama; **PARAGUAY:** PC World Paraguay; **P. R. OF CHINA:** China Computerworld, China Infoworld, Computer & Communication, Electronic Product World, Electronics Today, Game Camp, PC World China, Popular Computer Week, Software World, Telecom Product World; **PERU:** Computerworld Peru, GamePro, PC World Profesional Peru, PC World Peru; **POLAND:** Computerworld Poland, Computerworld Special Report, Macworld, Networld, PC World Komputer; **PHILIPPINES:** Computerworld Philippines, PC Digest, Publish in Asia; **PORTUGAL:** Cerebro/PC World, Correio Informático/Computerworld, Mac•In/PC•In Portugal; **PUERTO RICO:** PC World Puerto Rico; **ROMANIA:** Computerworld Romania, PC World Romania, Telecom Romania; **RUSSIA:** Computerworld Rossiya, Network World Russia, PC World Russia; **SINGAPORE:** Computerworld Singapore, PC World Singapore, Publish in Asia; **SLOVENIA:** MONITOR; **SOUTH AFRICA:** Computing S.A., Network World S.A., Software World; **SPAIN:** COMUNICACIONES WORLD, Dealer World, Macworld España, PC World España; **SWEDEN:** CAP&Design, Computer Sweden, Corporate Computing, MacWorld, Maxi Data, MikroDatorn, Nätverk & Kommunikation, PC/Aktiv, PC World, Windows World; **SWITZERLAND:** Computerworld Schweiz, Macworld Schweiz, PCtip; **TAIWAN:** Computerworld Taiwan, Macworld Taiwan, PC World Taiwan, Publish Taiwan, Windows World; **THAILAND:** Thai Computerworld, Publish in Asia; **TURKEY:** Computerworld Monitör, MACWORLD Turkiye, PC WORLD Turkiye; **UKRAINE:** Computerworld Kiev, Computers & Software Magazine, PC World Ukraine; **UNITED KINGDOM:** Acorn User, Amiga Action, Amiga Computing, Amiga, Appletalk, CD Powerplay, CD-ROM Now, Computing, Connexion, GamePro, Lotus Magazine, Macaction, Macworld, Open Computing, Parents and Computers, PC Home, PC Works, The WEB; **UNITED STATES:** Cable in the Classroom, CD Review, CIO Magazine, Computerworld, Computerworld Client/Server Journal, Digital Video Magazine, DOS World, Electronic, InfoWorld, I-Way, Macworld, Maximize, MULTIMEDIA WORLD, Network World, PC World, PUBLISH, SWATPro Magazine, Video Event, WebMaster; **URUGUAY:** PC World Uruguay; **VENEZUELA:** Computerworld Venezuela, GamePro, PC World Venezuela; and **VIETNAM:** PC World Vietnam. 10/17/95b

Acknowledgments

Thanks to everyone who helped make this book possible, especially Leon Shklar, who got me hooked on Perl, and Bob Allen, who suggested I read about CGI. Thanks also to Russell Sellars and Dennis Egan, who paved the way for my return to research; Sue Dumais for creating the intellectual environment that fostered this book; Rich Miller for involving me in the Bellcore External Web Team (www.bellcore.com); and Larry Stead for the guitar that got me through the lonely nights. Thanks also to Sid Dalal, Karen Kukich, Gardner Patton, Paul Tukey, Dan Ketchum, Deborah Schmitt, Carol Lochbaum, and everyone else in Bellcore's Applied Research Area who has been so helpful to me during the crunch times.

I'd also like to thank Glenn Silverstein, who convinced me to come to Bellcore; Larry Lefkowitz, who always finds time to listen to my wild ideas; Adam Irgon, who hired me at Bellcore and supported me throughout; Simon Blackwell, who showed me what a first-rate consultant can do; plus Ik Yoo, Doris Ip, and everyone else I've had the pleasure of working with at Bellcore.

Thanks to everyone at IDG, including Amy Pedersen, my acquisitions manager; Bill Sullivan, whose unfailing dedication to this book made it really happen; Carol Henry, who did a fantastic job with the manuscript edit; Charlie Scott at outer.net who ran my code and kept me honest; and my reviewers and endorsers.

I also want to thank my family, including my brother, John, who convinced me that my ideas were worth pursuing; my parents, who have always been behind me 100%; and my brother-in-law Fred Pisani, who donated his time and advice when I needed them. Thanks everyone.

I'd also like to thank John R. Anderson in the Psychology Department at CMU, who gave me my first real programming job. Thanks also to Herb Simon for getting me interested in Artificial Intelligence; Elaine Kant for getting me through my first book; and all the other wonderful people in the CMU Computer Science Department.

I'd also like to give special thanks to Jim Spohrer and David Littman for steering me in the right direction when I was at Yale. You were there when I needed help the most. I can never repay you.

(The publisher would like to give special thanks to Patrick J. McGovern, without whom this book would not have been possible.)

Credits

**Senior Vice President
and Group Publisher**
Brenda McLaughlin

Acquisitions Manager
Gregory S. Croy

Acquisitions Editor
Amorette Pedersen

Brand Manager
Melisa M. Duffy

Managing Editor
Andy Cummings

Administrative Assistant
Laura J. Moss

Editorial Assistant
Tracy Brown

Production Director
Beth Jenkins

Production Assistant
Jacalyn L. Pennywell

**Supervisor of
Project Coordination**
Cindy L. Phipps

Supervisor of Page Layout
Kathie S. Schnorr

**Supervisor of Graphics
and Design**
Shelley Lea

Reprint Coordination
Tony Augsburger
Theresa Sánchez-Baker
Todd Klemme

Blueline Coordinator
Patricia R. Reynolds

Development Editor
William Sullivan

Manuscript Editor
Carol Henry

Technical Reviewer
Charlie Scott

Project Coordinator
Valery Bourke

Graphics Coordination
Gina Scott
Angela F. Hunckler

Media/Archive Coordination
Leslie Popplewell
Melissa Stauffer
Jason Marcuson

Production Page Layout
E. Shawn Aylsworth
Cheryl Denski
Mark Owens
Anna Rohrer

Proofreaders
Melissa Buddendeck
Michael Bolinger
Nancy Price
Robert Springer
Karen Gregor-York

Indexer
Sharon Hilgenberg

Book Design
Liew Design

Table of Contents

Introduction

This is an exciting time to be writing a book about programming CGI in Perl. The Common Gateway Interface (CGI) has become the standard way of building applications for the Internet's World-Wide Web. Simultaneously, the Perl programming language has emerged as a popular choice for CGI scripting. Perl 5.0 is Larry Wall's latest version of the Perl language — and it is impressive. Perl 5 offers object-oriented programming, reusable program modules, a generalized database interface, and the ability to embed your programs within C or C++ code. Some version of Perl is probably already available on your computer; if not, it is easy to install and costs nothing. Perl has a comprehensive international program archive and a support network of dedicated individuals around the world. It is no wonder that Perl 5 is quickly becoming industry's choice for building applications on the Web.

This introduction explains why Web fever is taking hold and why it matters to you. It gives an overview of the book content, tells who should be reading it, and how it is organized. It also includes the basic information you'll need to know before getting started with the programming examples. We hope you find this book informative and easy to read.

Backdrop

The Web is the fastest growing segment of the Internet with over 10 million users — and it is doubling in size every few months. With an international communications network, widely available free software, and accepted publishing standards, the Web is becoming *the* place to be in cyberspace.

It is now possible to become an author, publisher, or information service company on the Web for little capital investment. For example, the cost of connecting into the Web is plummeting as companies offering local phone service, long distance, and cable get into the business of providing Internet service. For $20.00 per month or less, you can get a PPP (Point-to-Point Protocol) account that will make your computer part of the global Internet using just your modem and a phone line. In many areas, you can now connect your business directly to the Internet 24 hours a day with a dedicated line, in much the same way that you ask for phone service. In the near future, you will be able to stream your message to millions of people around the world for about the cost of a business phone line. With the growth of ISDN, frame relay, ATM, fiber optics, and other high-bandwidth communications technologies, you will be able to send more information over the Internet than ever before. Full-color high-resolution advertisements for your business, conversations with your friends and associates, video segments from news and entertainment programs, and software programs are just a sample of what can be accessed over the Internet.

The wide availability of free Web browsers like Mosaic, Netscape Navigator, and Internet Explorer have made surfing the Web cheaper and easier than ever before. Java, VRML, and real-time audio and video conferencing software are making the Web-surfing experience more enjoyable every day.

You will soon find Web software bundled with the computers you buy, the electronic appliances you own, and the desktop PC software you use every day. The information base to which you have direct access will become much larger, encompassing all of the information available on the global Internet.

HTML is now an accepted Internet publishing standard. HTML makes it easy to create and link information across the world. There are now numerous books available for people wanting to publish on the Web. There are also a growing number of books that explain how to set up and maintain a Web site. Many companies offer home page and Web site hosting services. You can even buy complete Internet solutions "in a box" that include the computer, software, and step-by-step instructions.

A growing number of Web sites are now offering more than just HTML. They are offering dynamic information services such as job searching, directory assistance, order tracking, help desks, on-line shopping, and more. These information services consist of software programs residing at the Web site that does the dirty work: creating the Web pages you see, processing on-line order forms, and searching databases.

About This Book

This book is targeted at the busy computer professional who wants to learn more about how to create Web-based application programs like those just mentioned. It explains CGI, a programming interface standard that allows you to connect your software program to the Web. It teaches you Perl, a popular computer language for writing Web-based software applications. It includes the code for an entire on-line shopping service written in object-oriented style using Perl 5.0.

We take you step-by-step through the process of creating many of the CGI programs you will need to create a top-notch Web site. We also point you to lots of on-line and print resources where you can learn more. This book is your one-stop shopping place for information related to CGI and Perl.

Should You Be Reading This Book?

Most users of the World-Wide Web will find this book informative, but it is primarily aimed at people who want to write programs to enhance their Web site. It gently introduces the reader to programming in Perl and includes numerous examples.

This book is a valuable resource for anyone wanting to add greater interactivity to their Web pages. It assumes a basic knowledge of HTML, but introduces the reader to advanced features like scripting and forms.

Computer professionals looking to get into the business of providing information services on the Web can use this book to gain a greater understanding of what is involved in creating Web-based services. Only a basic understanding of the Internet and programming concepts is required to read many of the chapters.

How This Book Is Organized

This book is divided into three Parts. Part I explains how the World-Wide Web works, how to use the CGI programming interface to Web server software packages, and how to get started programming with CGI — using the Perl language.

Part II takes you step-by-step through the most common types of CGI programs. All examples are in Perl. Relevant Perl statements are explained as they are used. We cover writing and debugging Perl CGI programs, generating dynamic Web pages, creating and processing forms, and adding search capabilities.

Part III provides a complete application using the code in Part II. It covers how to design applications for the Web using the example of an on-line shopping service. We guide you step-by-step through the process of creating this service, including HTML pages, Perl 5 code, and a sample product database. Then, we examine how to make Web applications secure from hackers. Finally, we look forward to emerging languages and approaches to Web application development with an eye towards forecasting future developments. The resource guide at the end of the book contains pointers to information sources for learning more about developing applications for the Web, plus a listing of Web sites that contain up-to-date information about CGI and Perl.

Before You Get Started

Although the CGI standard is platform-independent and the Perl language assumes no particular platform, most Web server software packages run on the UNIX platform and Perl was first implemented on UNIX. Therefore, the examples in this book were implemented on a UNIX platform (Sun Solaris 2.5). However, no knowledge of UNIX is required to use this book.

The examples in this book were tested using the NCSA HTTP server software, a widely available and free Web server software package. However, the examples in this book should run on a wide variety of popular Web servers.

Most examples in this book work in both Perl 4.0 (patch level 36) and 5.0 (patch level 1 or better). However, we include valuable tips for utilizing Perl 5 features to create better CGI programs.

Part One

The World-Wide Web, CGI, and Perl

Here in Part I we'll cover the basic concepts behind the World-Wide Web. You'll find out what you need to know to get started building Web applications in Perl.

Chapter 1 gives an overview of the Web. It introduces the exciting developments happening right now, as well as the potential for delivering applications across the Internet. It explains terms you've probably already encountered — URL, HTML, CGI, and more.

In Chapter 2, you'll find out how Web programming actually works. We'll introduce the CGI programming interface and explain why it's important that you master it before you start building Web-based applications.

Chapter 3 covers the Perl programming language. You'll see why it is a popular choice for writing CGI programs. Perl is available free of charge, and we'll explain how to download it and get it running. When you're done with Chapter 3, you'll be ready to start building CGI programs that will create dynamic Web pages, respond to user input, and provide searching capabilities.

Chapter 1

The World-Wide Web

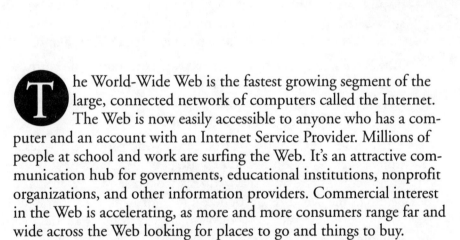

T he World-Wide Web is the fastest growing segment of the large, connected network of computers called the Internet. The Web is now easily accessible to anyone who has a computer and an account with an Internet Service Provider. Millions of people at school and work are surfing the Web. It's an attractive communication hub for governments, educational institutions, nonprofit organizations, and other information providers. Commercial interest in the Web is accelerating, as more and more consumers range far and wide across the Web looking for places to go and things to buy.

Until very recently, the Web was primarily used as an information repository, where users deposited documents for other users to find and use. The Common Gateway Interface (CGI) lets you go beyond the medium of static documents. With CGI you can accept input from users, search databases across the Internet, and respond immediately to the user's choices. Such capabilities enable companies to automate the flow of information among discrete work sites; allow consumers to buy goods and services in global electronic shopping malls; and help publishers to offer Web-based news and magazines where you can read about the latest developments around the world.

3

What Makes Up the World-Wide Web

This chapter explains the basic components of the World-Wide Web.

- *Web Browsers:* Web access software that runs on your computer. Modern browsers provide an interactive multimedia experience for the user. Web browsers may eventually comprise your TV, radio, telephone, and reference library—all rolled into one easy-to-use software package.

- *Web Sites:* Places to go on the Web. Web sites are maintained by companies, government agencies, schools—maybe even your friend down the street.

- *Web Documents:* Files of information residing at a Web site. These documents can include *hyperlinks* to information at other Web sites. Select a link, and you are immediately taken to another part of the Web without having to type in any special commands.

- *Web Servers:* Software that runs at a Web site and then returns information resources to Web browsers upon request. Web servers wait for users to request information resources and then return the requested information immediately.

- *Gateway Programs:* Software that accepts and processes requests from a Web server on behalf of a user, and generates new Web documents in return. Users' requests are typically for a program to be run at the Web site, or for access to information services somewhere on the Internet. A whole world of electronic mail, databases, newsgroups, and chat rooms are available on the Web because gateway programs are providing the connections to this stream of information. Gateway programs add a new level of interactivity not possible with broadcast media and traditional on-line references.

Anyone can add information to the Web and link it to related information across the globe. This global hyperlinking is what weaves the Web, making it possible for other users to see how you've connected things together.

After you are done with this chapter, you will understand how the Web works, how individuals and companies are using the Web, and why a gate-way program is an important element of nearly every winning Web site.

Web Browsers

You've probably already viewed documents on the Web using a *Web browser* such as Netscape Navigator or Microsoft Internet Explorer. When you're using a Web browser, it doesn't matter whether the document you're viewing on screen is stored on the machine in your basement or one in Hong Kong—the document will look the same to you. Figure 1-1 shows *HotWired*'s home on the Web, in the Netscape browser.

Web browsers make it feasible to quickly jump around the world looking for information on a particular subject. You can use your Web browser to read newspapers and magazines, shop for products and services, get in touch with people who share your interests, and to help you work faster.

Web browsers differ in their particular features, but they all support ways of specifying exactly the Web resource you want to display; they all handle multimedia information; and they all support hyperlinks. Let's take a look at each of these features. Then we'll examine the most popular Web browsers on the market today.

Specifying Web Resources to Display

A *Web resource* is a file of information that resides at a Web server machine. All of the resources available through your Web browser have a *Web address* or a *Uniform Resource Locator* (or URL, pronounced by saying the letters, *U R L* or by saying the word *earl*) so you can easily find them.

There are URLs for Web sites as well as the various Web documents stored at these sites. Web browsers typically allow you to type in URLs to go directly to a Web resource, for the fastest route to and the most up-to-the-minute version of what you need.

Just as there is a standard way of writing zip codes and phone numbers, there is a standard way of writing Web addresses. The URL tells the Web server software exactly where to find the resource and how to transfer it to your computer. URLs are quickly becoming as ubiquitous as phone numbers and e-mail addresses. They are showing up in TV commercials, TV program credits, print advertisements in magazines, and on business cards.

Figure 1-1: *HotWired's* home on the Web, shown in Netscape

We'll examine the format of URLs more thoroughly in a later section of this chapter.

Now let's look at how to specify the URLs for Web sites and individual Web documents.

Web Site URLs

Each Web site has its own URL. For example, *HotWired* magazine's
URL is

```
http://www.hotwired.com
```

  Big organizations on the Internet may have more than one Web site
URL, but most companies like to advertise their *home page* as a starting point. Home page URLs do not necessarily correspond to company names, but they often do.

  For a list of home pages, you can go to an on-line Internet directory
such as Yahoo!, one of the most popular and useful sites on the Web:

```
http://www.yahoo.com
```

Individual Document URLs

After you have located a Web site, you may need to find individual
documents at that site. You can directly address these documents using
slightly longer URLs. For example, to view a useful style guide document just type in this long URL:

```
http://www.w3.org/pub/WWW/Provider/Overview.html
```

Handling Multimedia Information

In 1991, the World-Wide Web was accessible only in textual form.
With the development of NCSA Mosaic in early 1993, browsers could
lay out both text and graphics on the same page. The Web now supports text, graphics, audio, video, and other media in a uniform and
extensible manner. The newest extensions are adding animation, 3-D
graphics, and plug-in multimedia add-ons to create an exciting and
multimodal Web surfing experience.

Graphics

The two most common formats for graphics on the Web are GIF
(CompuServe's Graphics Interchange Format) and JPEG (Joint
Photographic Experts Group). GIF supports 256 colors per image and
is good for line drawings and simple graphics. JPEG supports 24-bit
color and is good for photographic images. PNG (Portable Network
Graphics) is a new format that promises to replace GIF as the standard
graphics format on the Web.

Audio and Video

Audio on the Web is usually 8-bit, which is good for voice and low-quality musical recordings. Microsoft Windows mainly supports the WAV format, Macintosh has the AIFF format, and UNIX supports the AU format. It is a good idea to provide sound files in each of these formats, because users browsing your Web pages may be using any of these platforms.

Video on the Web is usually in Motion Pictures Expert Group's MPEG, Apple's QuickTime, or Intel's Indeo (Video for Windows) format. QuickTime and Indeo support synchronized audio and video; MPEG supports video only. Video is not used extensively on the Web because it often takes too long to download.

Animation

Web browsers not only incorporate multiple media, but they can display combinations of these media simultaneously. Sun's Java language

```
http://java.sun.com
```

can support simultaneous audio and animations on Web pages. A large collection of interesting Java programs (applets) can be found at

```
http://www.gamelan.com
```

3-D Graphics

Using VRML (Virtual Reality Modeling Language) you can add 3-D graphics to Web pages; see

```
http://vrml.wired.com
```

Plug-Ins

Some browsers, including Netscape Navigator 2.0, support multimedia plug-in software. This allows third-party developers to create programs that run on your desktop and appear within your Web browser page. There are plug-ins for embedding slide shows, spreadsheets, and other "live" information.

Hyperlinking

Using a Web document editor, you can create Web pages that other users can view in their Web browsers. You can add *hyperlinks* between the text or graphics on one page and the text or graphics on another page. When users read your document in a Web browser, they can select hyperlinks with their pointing device or keyboard. The Web browser automatically moves to another part of the current page or another page altogether, as specified by the hyperlink. Hyperlinks are the mainstay of the Web; they make it easy to jump from topic to topic. It's easy to get addicted.

Modern Web browsers support *hypermedia* by allowing hyperlinks among various types of media. This means you can click on a graphic and hear a sound clip, or click on a segment of text and move to another page with an animation sequence. Don't go off the deep end, though—keep your hypermedia designs simple so that users know what to expect.

Popular Browsers

Web browsers are generally inexpensive or free and available on a wide range of platforms. Following are descriptions of a few of the most popular ones.

Mosaic

Mosaic is the original "killer app" from NCSA (National Center for Supercomputing Applications) that made the World-Wide Web so popular. Version 2 is available for UNIX, the Macintosh, and Windows 3.1. You can download Mosaic from

```
http://www.ncsa.uiuc.edu/SDG/Software/Mosaic/
```

For an excellent introduction to Mosaic, check out *Mosaic for Dummies* from IDG Books Worldwide, Inc.

Note: When no document is specified, most Web servers will automatically transfer the user to an *index document*, such as *index.html*. Thus, the preceding URL for Mosaic is equivalent to *http://www.ncsa.uiuc.edu/SDG/Software/Mosaic/index.html*

Netscape Navigator

Netscape Navigator from Netscape Communications Corporation is currently the most popular Web browser. This popular software package is free and includes support for in-line multimedia plug-ins, Java applets, integrated e-mail, and newsgroups. See

```
http://www.netscape.com/comprod/products/navigator/
```

You can purchase documentation and support separately. Another IDG book, *Netscape for Dummies,* describes Netscape in detail.

Note: Many pages you'll find on the Web can only be viewed using a Netscape browser.

Microsoft Internet Explorer

Microsoft Internet Explorer is quickly becoming a formidable competitor for Netscape Navigator. See

```
http://www.microsoft.com/ie/
```

Microsoft also plans to offer Visual Basic Script, plus custom OLE (Object Linking and Embedding) controls to support multimedia plug-ins.

Additional Browsers

There are now over 50 Web browsers available for a wide range of platforms. Look for AIR Mosaic, Enhanced Mosaic, and Quarterdeck Mosaic for Windows 3.1; and MacMosaic and MacWeb for the Macintosh.

Internet World's 60 Minute Guide to the Internet, another book in the *60 Minute* series from IDG Books, includes a demo version of the Open Text Enhanced Mosaic Web browser.

Special Web browsers are also available from major on-line services, including CompuServe, America Online, and Prodigy. (Many on line services also support Netscape Navigator or Microsoft Internet Explorer). Users will have more choices than ever as the battle heats up for control of the Internet browser market and Internet-enabled PC desktop.

Finding and Managing Web Resources

Over 80,000 Web sites were available on the World-Wide Web as of January 1, 1996, and the number is doubling every few months! Nearly all educational, government, and commercial institutions now have a presence on the Web. You can visit their home pages to find out what products or services are being offered, who works there, and more.

Table 1-1 is a short list of some diverse Web sites, including their home page URL. Surf these sites—you'll find documents describing everything from quarterly reports to famous practical jokes.

Table 1-1: Some Web Sites You May Want to Visit

WEB SITE	HOME PAGE URL
PC Magazine	http://www.zdnet.com/pcmag
IBM	http://www.ibm.com
U.S. House of Representatives	http://www.house.gov
Carnegie-Mellon University	http://www.cmu.edu
NBC	http://www.nbc.com

Search Facilities

Finding specific resources on the Web is usually a lot more difficult than finding phone numbers in the Yellow Pages. There are millions of individual resources on the Web—and no single directory to find them. You can, however, use a combination of the popular *Internet-wide searching services,* search facilities at particular Web sites, and your browser's *Web page search facilities* to quickly zero in on the information you want to find.

Internet-wide Searching Services

To find documents located at diverse Web sites, you'll need to use an Internet-wide searching service. One good example of this type of service is Digital Equipment Corporation's AltaVista Search Engine:

```
http://www.altavista.digital.com
```

To find the URLs for documents at Web sites located around the world, you just type in a word or phrase and start the search. Click on the URL you want to visit, and the Web browser takes you right to the proper Web page.

Web Site Search Facilities

Web sites usually provide a search facility to find individual documents at the site. Look at the top or bottom of the company home page to see if a search facility is available.

With the large number of free, top-notch search engine software packages available, there is no reason why every site on the Web can't have a search facility. In Chapter 8, Adding Search Capabilities, you will see examples of good search facilities and learn how to create this kind of service for your Web site.

Web Page Search Facilities

Most Web browsers provide a facility for searching for a particular word or phrase within a particular Web document. Look at your Web browser documentation for instructions about this feature.

Hot Lists and Bookmark Files

Web browsers let you maintain a *hot list* of favorite URLs that you can access easily. Instead of typing in long URLs time after time, you can select an assigned name from your own private listing of useful Web resources.

Most Web browsers allow you to save your hot list in a *bookmark file*. Bookmark files are really just Web documents that contain URLs for the Web resources you have decided to store away for later reference. Netscape Navigator 2.0, Air Mosaic, and other browsers allow you to arrange these Web resources into categories for easy reference. You can trade these files with your friends and coworkers.

Rating Services

Another tool you might want to consider is a Web resource rating service like that available from Point Communications:

```
http://www.point.com
```

This company maintains a listing of the top-rated 5% of all Web sites. You add your address to a subscription list, and receive e-mail when interesting new Web sites are rated highly.

Looking Ahead

Desktop software integration efforts are underway at Microsoft, IBM, and other companies. Soon you may be able to launch an Internet search from your favorite desktop software package, grab information from a Web site in Australia, and use it immediately in your brochure, checkbook, or company ledger.

Ultimately, all of the documents, software programs, television shows, newspapers, and other information will appear as though they are immediately available on your desktop. Internet-enabled computers and hand-held devices will subsume the television, telephone, newspapers, magazines, and other forms of communication. The time to be getting your message on the Web is *now*. When the technology matures, you'll be able to broadcast your message in several different ways across the world.

URLs: Uniform Resource Locators

Here's another January 1996 statistic: At that time, there were over one million pages of information on the Web—that means *billions* of individual words! With all of this information available, the ability to reference each document with a unique name becomes critical. This is the motivation behind URLs. URLs provide a uniform addressing scheme for retrieving most of the information available on the Internet through a Web browser.

In this section, we'll dissect the format of the URL standard, breaking it into pieces and examining each part.

Sample URL

Here is a URL for a document that describes the winners of the National Information Infrastructure awards:

```
http://www.att.com/net/nii.html
```

This URL conforms to the following format for many *http* URLs on the Web:

```
protocol://host/path
```

Let's take a look at the elements of this format.

The Protocol Part of the URL

The first part of a URL is the *protocol,* and it's usually *http.* A protocol is just a set of rules for two computers to use when transferring data.

The *http* tells you that this is a URL for a resource available through a Web browser and will be transferred using the HTTP (HyperText Transfer Protocol) messaging scheme. There are numerous other Internet protocols, including FTP (File Transfer Protocol), gopher (menus of files), and mailto (e-mail).

HTTP specifies which messages the Web browser client (for instance, Netscape Navigator) and the Web server software (for instance, Netscape Commerce Server) should use to communicate. Using this protocol, the Web server will send the contents of the Web resource to the user for viewing. The rest of the URL designates the actual file to be sent and where it resides.

The Host Part of the URL

After the protocol name *(http)* and two forward slashes (*//*) comes the *Internet domain name* of the Web server machine or host (in our example, *www.att.com*).

Getting a Domain Name

An organization called the InterNIC processes requests for new domain names. Domain names are inexpensive to buy and maintain. Your local Internet Presence Provider (IPP) can get a domain name for your computer if you don't already have one. The IPP can also set up a *virtual host* for you, letting you have a domain name without the cost of having your own Web server machine. To find an IPP near you, see

```
http://thelist.com
```

Read domain names from right to left. In our National Information Infrastructure example, the parts are as follows:

- The *com* domain means this is a company.

- The *att* says that this is a machine at AT&T.

- The *www* is the usual name for a machine running a Web site (though this is usually really an alias for the real name of the machine).

Sometimes you'll see an IP (Internet Protocol) address instead of the domain name in a URL; as far as the browser is concerned, they are equivalent. Each IP address consists of four numbers separated by periods. The IP address of *www.att.com* is 192.20.239.135.

The Path Part of the URL

The last part of the URL, */net/nii.html* in our example, is the path to the requested file. This path is much like the directory path to a file in the UNIX operating system. In this case, the file is a document, *nii.html,* in the */net* directory. The extension *.html* gives us a hint that this is a Web hypertext document.

Note: The path in a URL is not really the document's location on the host machine; it is a logical shorthand for the physical path on the machine. For example, the directory */net* is probably located wherever the Web server software is installed (*/etc/httpd/htdocs/net,* for instance).

Specifying an Optional Internet Port

In addition to the protocol, the Web server and Web browser must agree on the Internet port. The various Internet services (e-mail, Web browsing, file transfer) use different Internet ports, so it is important to get the right one for the service you are using.

The standard port numbers for Internet services range from 1 to 1,024. Port 80 is reserved for Web services, such as HTTP protocol conversations, but you can specify other ports using the following format:

```
protocol://host:port/path
```

Typically, you must have special privileges on a server machine to run a service on a port below number 1,024, so some Web servers run on higher ports (up to 65,535). For example, you can access the Student Information Processing Board at MIT with the following URL:

```
http://www.mit.edu:8001/
```

More than one Web server may run on a given computer system. Each server establishes a Web site and can return specific Web resources to users.

When the port is omitted, as in the following URL:

```
http://www.att.com
```

then port 80 is assumed, so normally you don't need to worry about ports.

URLs for Other Types of Web Resources

The World-Wide Web allows you to access much more than just hypertext documents. You can use your Web browser to download software files, view newsgroups, send e-mail, and run programs on the Web server machine. For these activities you will specify a URL, just as you do to access documents—but these URLs have a different format. The most frequently used URL formats are in Table 1-2.

Table 1-2: Some Internet Protocols and Their URL Formats

PROTOCOL	DESCRIPTION	URL FORMAT
File	Retrieve a document on local machine	*file://host/path*
FTP	Transfer files from remote machine	*ftp://user:passwd@host:port/path* Default port: 21
Gopher	List directory structure of remote machine	*gopher://host:port/path* Default port: 70
HTTP	Transfer Web resources such as HTML documents	*http://host:port/path* Default port: 80
Mailto	Send mail to user with Internet address	*mailto:name@host*
News	Retrieve USENET news articles	*news:newsgroup* OR *news:messageID*
Telnet	Start an interactive session	*telnet://user:password@host:port* Default port: 23
WAIS	Search a WAIS database	*wais://host:port/database* Default port: 210

HTML: HyperText Markup Language

HTML (HyperText Markup Language) is the electronic publishing format for hypertext documents on the Web. A *markup language* is just a set of codes or *tags* that specify how to format a document when it is displayed. In HTML, the codes specify the format for headings, lists, and other elements of Web documents, as well as how to embed hyperlinks to other documents. Tim Berners-Lee invented HTML while he was at Conseil Euròpen pour la Recherche Nuclèaire (CERN) in Switzerland. It has become a popular publishing language for the Web because it's readable, concise, and easy to learn.

Most popular word processing programs use a proprietary markup language. In contrast, HTML is an open standard managed by the Web consortium and the IETF (Internet Engineering Taskforce). The standardization of hypertext markup has made possible the viewing, sharing, and linking of documents across the world on the World-Wide Web.

This section discusses existing versions of HTML and various extensions. People across the world are using HTML to create home pages and other documents.

Versions of HTML

Three versions of HTML are currently in use: HTML/1.0, HTML/2.0, and HTML/3.0. To find out what version your browser supports, check your browser documentation.

HTML/1.0 and Semantic Markup

HTML/1.0 provides basic formatting capabilities. These capabilities are quite different from formatting codes used in popular word processing programs. In word processing, you use *physical markup* to specify exactly how the text should look. For example, you might specify a bold font and 14-point type size. In HTML, you use *semantic markup* to specify what the text means. That is, you *tag* the document with the proper HTML codes, and the Web browser displays the tagged text as it sees fit.

For example, the HTML tag <EM> says that the upcoming text should have added emphasis. When a Web surfer views this page using a browser, the browser may interpret the emphasis tag as italic. Another browser may render the emphasis in a different way—in a larger type size or brighter color, for example. Although browsers can run on a variety of platforms having different available fonts, with or without graphics, the HTML remains the same.

HTML/2.0 and Forms

HTML/2.0 is now an official IETF standard. This version of the HTML language offers support for fill-out forms. Forms provide a standard user interface for Web information services. They allow users to enter information such as name, phone number, and e-mail address into fields. Forms also support menus with check boxes and radio buttons for specifying options. Users fill out a form and then press a button to submit the data on the form to the Web server machine.

To make a form work, you need to include the required HTML/2.0 codes in your document, and you must write a CGI program to specify how the Web service should process the form's data. We will see how to do this in Chapter 6, Processing Forms.

HTML/3.0

HTML/3.0 offers a wealth of new features, including support for figures, tables, and mathematical equations. For instance, you can make text flow around a figure.

HTML/3.0 is still a draft, but its features are already supported by a number of browsers, including Enhanced Mosaic and Netscape Navigator 2.0. Netscape Navigator also supports several extensions to HTML/3.0, giving authors even greater control in rendering documents. Using these extensions, you can set font sizes and give more precise layout instructions. You can also divide your Web page into multiple subwindows using frames and toolbars.

You can get a complete description of HTML codes on the Web at

```
http://www.w3.org/pub/WWW/MarkUp/MarkUp.html
```

In addition, numerous books are available on HTML, including *HTML For Dummies* from IDG Books.

Web Server Software Packages

For a Web site to provide Web browsers with the documents they request, the host computer must run Web server software. Many versions are available today for a variety of platforms. This section explains how Web servers work and tells you where on the Internet you can find them.

Web Server Features

Web server software packages have a variety of features, but most support CGI scripting, APIs, server-side includes, and standard access log files.

CGI scripting

CGI scripts are programs that you supply. They are run by a Web server. This book describes many different types of CGI scripts and how to create them using the Perl programming language — by far the simplest and most inexpensive way to make your Web pages more interesting and interactive.

APIs

Some Web server software packages also support an Application Programming Interface (API). Using an API, you can compile your program directly with the Web server software for increased speed.

Server-Side Includes

Most Web server software packages allow you to embed special codes in your HTML documents. These *server-side includes* (SSIs) enable you to

- Include other Web pages in the current page
- Launch CGI scripts directly from a Web page
- Incorporate output from a CGI script directly into your Web page

All of this can happen in the brief time between the user's request for your Web page and when the page is actually viewed.

Chapter 5, Generating Dynamic Web Pages explores server-side includes; you'll see how to do lots of neat things—with little in the way of programming.

Standard Log Files

Web server software packages save a history of all requests to the Web server in a special *access log file.* You can print out this log file or write programs to collect information about customers who visit your site. For more details about the format of these files, consult a Web server book like *Build a Web Site* from Prima Online.

A variety of CGI scripts are available on the Web to automatically process log files, display them as graphs, and so on.

Popular Products

All of the original Web server software packages were developed for the UNIX operating system. Today, however, Web servers are available for many computing platforms, including Windows 3.1, Windows 95, Windows NT, and Apple Macintosh.

CERN HTTPd for UNIX

All of the Web server software packages mentioned in this book are based on the original server, created at CERN and called CERN HTTPd, the CERN HyperText Transfer Protocol daemon. (See sidebar, "HTTP Server Daemons and HTTP.")

NCSA HTTPd for UNIX

NCSA simplified and improved the CERN server to produce the first widely used Web server on the Internet. NCSA HTTPd is small, fast, easy to install, and free. To download the latest version, visit

```
http://hoohoo.ncsa.uiuc.edu/docs/Overview.html
```

and follow the instructions.

HTTP Server Daemons and HTTP

A *daemon* is a program that runs continually, waiting for events to happen. When an event occurs, the daemon wakes up and responds. This is how Web server software works. It runs on a given Internet port, waiting for connections from client programs, such as Web browsers. When a client connects, the server processes the request and goes back to waiting.

Netscape Communications Corporation Servers

Netscape Communications Corporation improved and commercial-ized the original NCSA server software. Netscape now offers a full line of Web servers, including the FastTrack Server, Communications Server, and Commerce Server . These servers are among the best rated on the market and many are free to nonprofit organizations. Prices have dropped dramatically since Microsoft and other companies have started offering similar products.

Secure Server Software

The Netscape Commerce Server and Microsoft Internet Information Server are *secure servers.* This means you can use them to receive credit card numbers and other sensitive information over the Internet from compatible Web browsers—without the fear of hackers intercepting the information as it travels across the Internet.

Any information input by users is scrambled by the Web browser into special encrypted codes before it is sent over the Internet to the Web server. The SSL (Secure Sockets Layer) protocol permits *only* a secure server to subsequently unscramble the message to get the decoded credit card number or other information. This doesn't prevent someone from looking over your shoulder or planting a program on your PC to capture this information, but it does prevent your number from being intercepted while its on its path over the Internet.

The Netscape servers provide reliable performance and come with good documentation and customer service. See

```
http://www.netscape.com/comprod/server_central/
```

for information on pricing and availability.

Microsoft Internet Information Server (IIS) for Windows NT

Microsoft Internet Information Server (IIS) is a free download. It is a full-featured server available for Windows NT (see sidebar, "Secure Server Software"). Go to

```
http://www.microsoft.com/infoserv
```

Other Server Software

Other Web server software packages that run on Windows NT include GNN from Global Network Navigator, Inc., and Purveyor from Process Software Corporation. Check *PC Magazine* or *Internet World* magazine for reviews of these popular packages.

Servers are also available for the Macintosh. MacHTTP for Macintosh systems is one of the easiest servers to install and configure. The commercial version of MacHTTP is called WebStar and is sold and supported by StarNine Technologies, Inc.:

```
http://www.starnine.com
```

You can now run a Web site on Windows 3.1 or Windows 95. Win-httpd from NCSA is basically a version of NCSA's HTTPd server that runs under Windows 3.1. Quarterdeck, O'Reilly, and other companies also offer good Web server packages that run on Windows 3.1 and Windows 95. Check with these companies for pricing and availability.

Server installation and administration vary somewhat on the different platforms. All of these Web servers support the CGI standard program interface, however, so Web programming across platforms is nearly identical.

CGI: The Common Gateway Interface

This section defines the Common Gateway Interface and explains its importance to Web programming.

What Is CGI?

The meaning of the phrase *Common Gateway Interface* can best be explained by defining each word.

- *Common* means widely applicable. In fact, CGI programs will work with all major Web server software packages.

- *Gateway* means a way of entry. CGI is a way for a world of information to enter the Web via your gateway program.

- *Interface* means the connection between two things. CGI will connect a Web server software package and your application program.

CGI specifies how the Web server software package sends information to external programs, as well as how these programs send information back. Your external CGI programs are also called *CGI scripts*.

Why Is CGI Important?

Companies are starting to realize that they can use the Web for more than just providing access to company information and advertising. Today any individual or company can offer innovative information services over the Web. We are seeing news, weather, sports, shopping, entertainment, travel, dating, employment, health, and legal services. CGI programs are at the heart of these information services.

Table 1-3 shows some examples of the kinds of services that are now available.

Table 1-3: Some of the Available Information Services

The Net Discount Mall	`http://www.ndm.com`	Check off the items you want on a simple order form. Call or e-mail your credit card information and you can get a member ID that you use on line.
JewelryNet	`http://www.infi.net/jewel`	Browse through a catalog of Southwest sterling silver jewelry; then order items of interest.
Accu-http: Weather	`//accuwx.com/`	Find out the current weather in your area or track storms as they develop.
Internet	`http://www.ird.net/`	Choose a restaurant and order your favorite items off the menu. You receive a tally, enter your current location and your credit card, and the food is delivered to your doorstep! Check for availability in your area.

You can create these kinds of information services at your Web site using the Common Gateway Interface. Using CGI, you can design gateways to Internet services, fill-in forms, and dynamic Web pages. Let's look at each of these.

Gateways to Internet Services

Gateway programs can provide access to a range of Internet facilities from your Web site, including e-mail, file transfer, chat rooms, and find information about someone on the Internet, using an e-mail address. The **finger** program already does this, so you create a CGI program that provides access to **finger** for your Web users. This is an example of a gateway program. It takes a request to run **finger** with a particular email address as an argument, and translates the request into the **finger** protocol. Your program then translates the output back into a form the Web user can read.

CGI was originally created to provide a common interface to gateway programs. You'll find out how to create these kinds of programs in Chapter 4, Creating CGI Programs.

Forms

Forms are the easiest and most familiar mechanism for passing data to information services. Forms are a kind of graphical user interface for Web pages that are employed for nearly any kind of user input. Web programmers use several common types of forms: order forms, comment forms, and interactive publication forms. All of these require CGI programs to process them.

Chapter 6, Processing Forms, and Chapter 7, Providing Informative Responses, discuss the creation and processing of these forms.

Dynamic Web Pages

Dynamic Web pages are web pages generated by a CGI program. You may want to generate dynamic Web pages for several reasons: to add interactivity to on-line publications; to target your documents to an individual user; to create displays of real-time data; or to display information retrieved from a database.

Chapter 5, Generating Dynamic web pages covers two important techniques for creating dynamic Web pages.

Let's Get Started

The World-Wide Web is an exciting medium for providing information and services to users across the world. After you master CGI and Perl, you will be ready to take on the challenge of programming searching services, on-line catalog services, and other Web site offerings of your own design. So let's move ahead to Chapter 2, where we examine the Common Gateway Interface in detail.

The Common Gateway Interface (CGI)

W hen users access a Web page by typing in a URL or following a hyperlink, they are usually retrieving a static page of information. The Common Gateway Interface (CGI) provides a way for you to create Web pages that are composed each time they are accessed by a user. Using CGI, you can create your own gateways to interactive multimedia information services, search facilities, e-mail, and databases, and make these gateway programs accessible from your Web site or home page.

This chapter tells you what you can do with CGI and details which Web server software packages and programming languages you need to get started. It explains the workings of CGI and addresses some potential concerns you might have with using it. You'll also find a detailed explanation of the CGI environment variables and techniques for getting the most out of your Web server, including how to use CGI programs to access input typed into HTML forms. After reading this chapter, you will be able to put CGI to work to fully exploit the Web's interactive capabilities.

Overview of CGI

CGI is not a programming language or data format—it is a standard programming interface to Web server software packages. It has generated significant interest in the Internet community and has already become widely adopted. CGI enables portability of application programs across Web server software packages, and even across different computing platforms. It works with a variety of programming languages, including Perl and Visual Basic. This flexibility has made CGI the most popular programming interface to today's Web server software packages.

Why Use CGI?

Prior to the CGI standard, each Web server program had its own way of running applications. This made it difficult for Web sites to share application programs. The CGI standard provides a uniform method for passing information to and from these applications.

Using CGI, you can

- Run programs provided by your Webmaster or Internet Service Provider. These may be simple CGI scripts that you can embed in your HTML documents, or they may be more sophisticated CGI programs that search databases, handle payments, or perform other common Web services.

- Run applications written by CGI programmers. These programs can register you in an on-line guest book, enable you to "chat" with other Internet users from across the Internet, and provide other common Web services.

- Run your own programs. You can install these programs on a Web server in a directory accessible by your Web server software and make them available to Web document authors at your Web site or to users across the Web. You instantly become the publisher of an Internet information service!

Think of CGI as your entry into a worldwide library of software. You can run someone else's program no matter where it is located, whether it's running on Windows or a Mac or any other operating system, and regardless of the programming language in which it is written.

Tip: Another advantage of using CGI is that many CGI programs can be downloaded from file server machines on the Internet, free of charge. It is easy to share and improve CGI software written by other programmers.

Web Server Support for CGI

CGI was created at NCSA, the National Center for Supercomputing Applications. Like much of the Web, CGI has a short history. NCSA released version 1.0 of CGI in 1992, followed by an enhanced version, 1.1. This chapter describes CGI/1.1.

Most Web server software packages support CGI/1.1, including the latest versions of CERN HTTPd, NCSA HTTPd, the Netscape Web servers, and Microsoft IIS. If you purchase a new Web server package such as NaviServer or Purveyor, it will have built-in support for CGI programming. Support among older Web servers varies; see Table 2-1.

Table 2-1: CGI Support in Older Web Server Software Packages

SERVER SOFTWARE	NOT SUPPORTING CGI/1.0	SUPPORTS CGI/1.0	SUPPORTS CGI/1.1
NCSA	Earlier than 1.0	1.0 and 1.1	1.2 and later
CERN	Earlier than 2.15	2.15, 2.16, 2.17	2.18 and later
Netscape	N/A	N/A	All versions

Programming Language Support for CGI

CGI allows you to create programs in any programming language. Most Web server software packages, however, recommend using a small number of programming languages:

- UNIX: a shell(**sh**, **csh**, or **ksh**), C, C++, and Perl.
- Apple Macintosh: HyperCard, AppleScript, and MacPerl (a Macintosh version of the Perl language).
- Microsoft Windows: Visual Basic and BigPerl, a version of the Perl language that runs on Windows 95, NT, and 3.1 (using 32-bit extensions).

Note: For the most recent developments in CGI's support for Web server software packages and programming languages, point your browser to the Web consortium's page on CGI, at *http://www.w3.org/pub/WWW/CGI/Overview.html*.

How CGI Works

To understand how CGI works, you need to know

- How to reference CGI programs as URLs so you can insert them into your Web pages and pass data to them

- How data input by users is transmitted between a Web browser and a Web server over the Internet

- How the Web server software runs your CGI program after it receives the proper data

How to Reference CGI Programs as URLs

The general format for URLs that run CGI programs is as follows:

```
http://host:port/path/program/extra?search
```

Here are explanations of the elements in any CGI URL:

- The *host* is the Web server machine where the CGI program resides.

- The *port* is the same port as for other HTTP requests, usually 80.

- The *path* is usually *cgi-bin,* but it could be any path to a directory where executable programs are stored.

- The *program* is the name of the CGI program, including any extensions (such as *.pl* or *.cgi*).

- The *extra* path information is usually a flag or switch passed to the CGI program (such as */debug*) or a path to a directory where program data can be found.

- The *search* part is where you can supply words and phrases to pass to a search facility. In practice, this element of the URL is where all kinds of data will be stored, including user input to HTML forms.

When these CGI URLs are embedded into HTML documents, users can run programs simply by selecting a labeled *hyperlink* on a Web page. An example of this embedding technique is given in Chapter 4.

When a user submits a form by clicking a button, the forms data is transmitted to a CGI program using the same URLs. This process is explained in Chapter 6.

How HTTP Transmits Data Over the Web

The HTTP protocol provides a common language for diverse software programs to communicate across the Internet. HTTP is used by all Web server software packages and Web client programs around the world. A *client program* (your Web browser, for example), running on a machine in your office in Boston, USA, can communicate with a *server program* (a Netscape Commerce Server, for example), running on a machine halfway around the world in Tokyo. In cyberspace, everybody speaks the same language!

Web server software (such as NCSA HTTPd or NaviServer) functions much like a centralized telephone switching station. It uses the HTTP protocol to connect client programs that "call up" the server machine, to information services available on that machine (CGI programs, for example). The client programs are Web browsers such as Netscape Navigator or Mosaic; Web "crawlers" that systematically search the Internet for information; and remote session manager programs such as **telnet**.

All of these client programs do the same thing—they ask for information from the Web server software. In turn, the Web server either "serves" that information directly to the client program, or calls a CGI program and then returns the output from that program back to the original client program.

Note: The current release, HTTP/1.0, is the first full release and is supported by all major Web server software packages. The earlier HTTP/0.9 only supported retrieving resources. HTTP/1.1 and HTTP/1.2 are currently draft documents. For the latest developments, go to *http://www.w3.org/pub/WWW/Protocols*.

The Advantages of HTTP

HTTP has three attributes that make it a great protocol for communication over the Internet.

1. It is *extensible*. HTTP uses special headers to send information describing the resources being transmitted. For instance, the HTTP header can indicate when a resource was last modified and by whom. Client programs can use this information to disregard very old resources, track modifications to resources, and so forth. For the server program, the header can provide the user's identity, what kinds of information the user can accept, and more.

2. It is *simple*. The HTTP protocol is connectionless—each request creates a new connection to the server machine. It is also stateless—no information is retained about the client program's state between requests.

3. It is *universal*. HTTP now accounts for more Web traffic than any other protocol, including FTP, **telnet**, and **gopher**. The flexibility, simplicity, and universal nature of HTTP has fueled the popularity of the World-Wide Web.

How HTTP Works

Hold on to your Web browser—we're going to try to explain how client and server programs communicate using HTTP.

HTTP is a simple protocol when compared with others, such as FTP and **gopher**. Figure 2-1 illustrates HTTP's five-step process.

1. The client program makes a connection to a server program over the Internet.

2. The client sends an HTTP request message to the server.

3. The server processes the request message, optionally using CGI programs.

4. The server sends back an HTTP response message.

5. The server closes the connection.

This process is repeated over and over again, every time you click on a hyperlink and go surfing off to some new Web site.

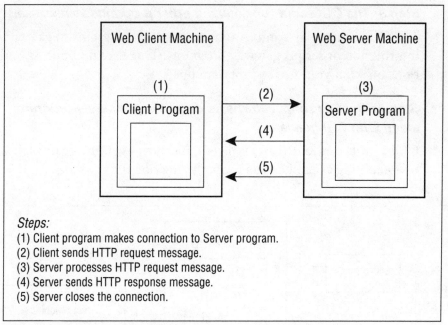

Steps:
(1) Client program makes connection to Server program.
(2) Client sends HTTP request message.
(3) Server processes HTTP request message.
(4) Server sends HTTP response message.
(5) Server closes the connection.

Figure 2-1: The steps of a client-server exchange using the HTTP protocol

How the Web Server Software Runs Your CGI Programs

When you run a CGI program over the Web (by selecting a hyperlink on the Web page, for example), you see the CGI program's output as though you have simply accessed a document or other Web resource. To achieve this result, the Web server software goes through a series of events to process the HTTP request and respond back to the client program with this resource. Here are these events, as illustrated in Figure 2-2.

Step 1: The HTTP server program receives an HTTP request from a client program

The server notes that the requested URL contains a reference to a CGI script.

Step 2: The server program sets variables and executes the CGI script

Some of the variables depend upon the type of HTTP request; others are always set.

Step 3: The CGI script runs, calling other programs as necessary

The CGI script may connect to remote server programs to gather information or scripts gateway programs. There are no built-in limitations on what your CGI scripts can do.

Step 4: The CGI script returns its output to the server program, along with CGI headers

CGI scripts can return any type of data, such as an image or plain text—as long as the headers properly describe the contents.

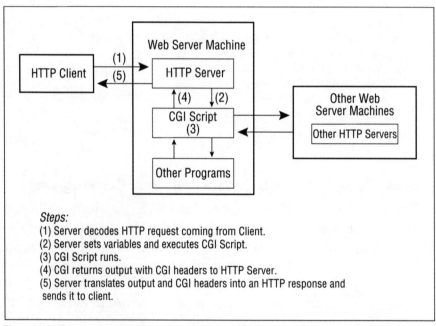

Steps:
(1) Server decodes HTTP request coming from Client.
(2) Server sets variables and executes CGI Script.
(3) CGI Script runs.
(4) CGI returns output with CGI headers to HTTP Server.
(5) Server translates output and CGI headers into an HTTP response and sends it to client.

Figure 2-2: The server program's steps to process an HTTP request with a CGI program.

Step 5: The server program translates the CGI output and headers into a valid HTTP response for the client

The output from the server program appears the same as any other resource. If the client program is a Web browser and the data returned is formatted as HTML, the user will see it as a normal Web page.

The Input to CGI Programs

Now that you understand how CGI works, let's look at how CGI programs get their input data from the HTTP server: from environment variables; from the standard input stream; and from the command line. Then we'll look at the different types of output that CGI programs can generate.

Getting Input from Environment Variables

Before CGI programs run, the Web server sets a number of *environment variables.* Environment variables are just like variables in a programming language, but instead of being accessible solely by the program that defines them, they are accessible in all programs called by the initial program. (See the sidebar, "Environment Variables.") Because the Web server is just another program that calls your CGI programs, the environment variables set by the Web server are accessible in your CGI programs.

In Chapter 5, we will see how to access the values of CGI environment variables using Perl.

Environment Variables

Environment variables are available in most operating systems. The UNIX environment variables include SHELL, which identifies the type of command interpreter you are running, and PATH, which specifies a list of directories to search for programs.

To list all of your environment variables, use the **printenv** command if you are using UNIX or the SET command if you are using DOS. Check your system documentation for the appropriate command on any other operating system.

In CGI programs, environment variables are used to obtain the following:

- User input typed into forms or hidden in the search part of a CGI URL

- The identity of the user and Internet address of the user's machine

- The name of the CGI program itself and its location on the Web server machine

33

- Information about the Web server program that referenced this CGI program
- Information contained in the headers of the HTTP request

Getting Information Supplied by Client Programs

This section describes the environment variables used for getting input to your CGI program from Web client programs. The most common variables in this category are REQUEST_METHOD, QUERY_STRING, CONTENT_LENGTH, and CONTENT_TYPE.

Caution: Environment variables are case sensitive, so be sure to use all capital letters as required. Also be sure to include the underscore characters between words.

REQUEST_METHOD

REQUEST_METHOD is set to one of two common values: GET and POST. This variable tells a CGI program about other variables that will contain the user's input.

- If REQUEST_METHOD is GET, your CGI program will get the user's input from the QUERY_STRING variable.
- If REQUEST_METHOD is POST, your program will read the user's input from the standard input stream, as if the user had typed input directly on the workstation. You can use the value in CONTENT_LENGTH to determine how many characters to read.

When using HTML forms, if you do not specify a REQUEST_METHOD, the value GET will be supplied by the Web server software.

GET Requests

The Web server sets QUERY_STRING to the *search* part of the URL—that is, anything after the first question mark. For example, in the following URL:

```
http://hoohoo.uiuc.ncsa.edu/cgi-bin/finger.pl?farrell@idgbooks.com
```

the search part of the URL is:

farrell@idgbooks.com

When processing forms, if the REQUEST_METHOD is GET, the HTTP server puts the entire contents of the filled-out form in the search part of the URL. Thus your CGI program can get the form contents from the QUERY_STRING variable.

Caution: Beware that servers typically have a maximum permitted length for a URL. For this reason, the POST method is often used when the amount of user input can't be determined ahead of time.

The content of QUERY_STRING is *URL-encoded.* This means that whatever the user inputs will be converted into a format easily digested by CGI programs. Each form element name and its corresponding value are separated by equal signs (=). Individual name/value pairs are separated by ampersands (&). Also, special characters are *escaped* (see sidebar, "Encoding Special Characters in URLs"). The result of URL-encoding is a string of characters like this one:

```
name=Rob%20Farrell&email=farrell%40idgbooks.com
```

Chapter 6 of this book provides a Perl software library that you can use to decode URLs, so you never have to work directly with these kinds of complex URL strings.

POST Requests

The CONTENT_LENGTH and CONTENT_TYPE variables are used with the POST request method. CONTENT_LENGTH tells your program how many characters of data to read.

Using the Perl software library we provide in Chapter 6, your program will receive the form data as a character string and won't have to worry about these environment variables.

Encoding Special Characters in URLs

Not all data can be passed to CGI programs without modification. Certain special characters are permitted in URLs, but others must be *escaped.* The rule for escaping a character is to take its value in ASCII, convert it to hexadecimal, and precede it with a percent sign (%). The following table lists the most common escaped characters and how to use them in URLs.

Don't worry about these escaped characters too much. The Perl software library we introduce in Part II knows how to "unescape" them for you.

ESCAPED CHARACTER	CODE	EXAMPLE
Tab	%09	col1%09col2
Newline	%0a	line1%0aline2
Space	%20	John%20Smith
@ (at sign)	%40	Smith%40rutgers.edu
& (ampersand)	%26	Smith%26Barney
? (question mark)	%3f	What%20is%20%20that%3f

Getting Information about the Client Program

This section lists the environment variables that provide useful information about the client program. You may want to use these variables to verify a user's identity or perform other security checks before allowing the user to run the rest of a CGI script.

REMOTE_ADDR

REMOTE_ADDR is the Internet Protocol (IP) address of the host making a connection to your Web server. You can use REMOTE_ADDR to verify that the connecting host is one that you want to run your program, or to send requested data back to this host.

REMOTE_HOST

The REMOTE_HOST variable is set to the domain name for the client host machine. This is a more meaningful name than the IP address for most uses. As an example, for a REMOTE_ADDR of 128.6.4.2 the REMOTE_HOST would be *aramis.rutgers.edu.*

You can also use the REMOTE_HOST variable to keep a log of client machines that are accessing your service.

REMOTE_IDENT

REMOTE_IDENT is the login name of the user, if one is available. You can use this variable to fill in forms but don't depend on it to reliably track users.

REMOTE_USER

REMOTE_USER is the login name the user provides when they are prompted for a name and password by their Web browser. You can use this information for gathering marketing data, doing direct advertising, or maintaining mailing lists. Bear in mind, however, that a recent survey showed that less than 20% of casual Web users were willing to provide their name when prompted.

AUTH_TYPE

The AUTH_TYPE, used for enhanced security, is the name of the scheme used for authenticating the user's identity. The only value supported in HTTP/1.0 is Basic, which is short for Basic User Authentication Scheme. See Chapter 11, on how to enhance security.

Getting Information About the CGI Program

This section lists the environment variables that store information about the CGI program itself and its location on the Web server machine. You can use this information to make scripts portable across Web servers, and to pass switches and other arguments to your scripts.

SCRIPT_NAME

The SCRIPT_NAME variable is set to the name of the CGI program (script) specified in the URL. This variable represents everything in the URL that comes after the host and port, up to and including the name of the executable CGI program. For example, in

```
http://hoohoo.ncsa.uiuc.edu/cgi-bin/test-cgi
```

the SCRIPT_NAME is *cgi-bin/test-cgi*.

SCRIPT_NAME is useful when a CGI program needs its own name. If you use this variable instead of the hard-coded name of the script, you can rename your CGI program without having to change your source code to reflect the new name. (It's really just a way for a CGI program to say "me".)

PATH_INFO

The PATH_INFO variable holds the value of the extra path information in the URL. This is the part of the URL following the name of the CGI program, but before the question mark. For example, in the URL

```
http://hoohoo.ncsa.uiuc.edu/cgi-bin/query.pl/trace?tag
```

the PATH_INFO is */trace.*

You can use PATH_INFO to pass other types of information to your CGI program besides what users enter in forms—say, a debugging switch or some tracing options.

Tip: In general, it's a good idea to make extra path information in URLs optional, so that HTML authors using your CGI program are not required to provide this information.

PATH_TRANSLATED

PATH_TRANSLATED is the directory path to the Web resource on the Web server machine. You can use this variable to print, save, or perform other operations on the file specified in the URL. If the URL is

```
http://hoohoo.ncsa.uiuc.edu/cgi-bin/query.pl/home.html
```

and Web server documents are stored in the directory /usr/local/etc/ httpd/htdocs, then PATH_TRANSLATED would be */usr/local/etc/ httpd/htdocs/home.html.*

Getting Information about the Web Server

This section lists the environment variables for getting information about the Web server software that is running your CGI script. You can use these variables to enhance the portability of your CGI programs.

SERVER_SOFTWARE

The SERVER_SOFTWARE variable allows you to identify which type of Web server software is running your CGI program—for instance, NCSA HTTPd/1.4.1.

SERVER_NAME and SERVER_PORT

SERVER_NAME and SERVER_PORT are the host name and port of the server machine that is calling your CGI program. Rather than hard-coding the name of the server or the port into your CGI program, it's best to use the values of these two variables. This will make it easier to move your program to other machines and Internet ports.

GATEWAY_INTERFACE

GATEWAY_INTERFACE gives the version of the CGI specification with which this server complies. To be robust, your CGI programs should check this variable. Newer versions of CGI should not invalidate your programs, but it's always wise to print a warning that your program is assuming an older version of the standard.

SERVER_PROTOCOL

SERVER_PROTOCOL is the name and revision of the Web protocol used in this HTTP request—almost always HTTP/1.0. To be robust, your CGI programs should check this variable because older versions of HTTP may not support the environment variables that you need in your CGI script.

Getting Information from the HTTP Headers

This section lists environment variables for getting information from the headers of the HTTP request message. The Web server can put any or all of the HTTP request headers into environment variables so they can be accessed directly by CGI programs.

Caution: Your CGI program should check to make sure these variables are set before using their values.

Each request header is placed in an environment variable with a prefix of HTTP_, followed by the header name. Any dashes (-) in the name are changed to underscores (_); thus, the User-Agent HTTP request header becomes HTTP_USER_AGENT. Let's take a look at the most common of these HTTP_ environment variables.

HTTP_USER_AGENT

The HTTP_USER_AGENT variable tells you the name of the client program accessed your Web server. The general format for this variable is *software/version*.

Caution: Not all browsers use the standard format for the HTTP_USER_AGENT variable. For example, if you are running Netscape Navigator 1.1 on a Sun workstation, HTTP_USER_AGENT will be set to something like this: `Mozilla 1.1/N (X11; I; SunOS 4.1.3 sun4m)`

You can use HTTP_USER_AGENT to track the types of browsers and other clients that access your site. You can also use this variable for customizing your CGI output to take advantage of extensions offered by some browsers without causing problems for others.

HTTP_REFERER

HTTP_REFERER tells you the URL for the Web page the user was on before your CGI program was run.

You can use HTTP_REFERER to keep profiles of which pages are generating the most "hits" (visits) for your Web site. You can also use this variable to create hyperlinks back to the index used to access your Web site (a hyperlink labeled "Back to Yahoo," for instance).

Caution: HTTP_REFERER will not be set when the user addresses your CGI program directly with a URL rather than hyperlinking to it from another Web page.

HTTP_FROM

The HTTP_FROM environment variable tells you the e-mail address of the user connecting to your server. Most modern Web browsers do not set this variable because it compromises the privacy of the user.

HTTP_ACCEPT

HTTP_ACCEPT tells you the MIME content types (covered later in this chapter) that are accepted by the browser running your CGI program. Here is the value of HTTP_ACCEPT from Netscape Navigator version 1.1:

```
*/*, image/gif, image/x-xbitmap, image/jpeg
```

You can use HTTP_ACCEPT in your CGI programs to figure out which media format you need to return to a particular Web browser. For example, if a browser accepts JPEG images, your CGI program could send photographic images in this format instead of the GIF format.

HTTP_ACCEPT_LANGUAGE

HTTP_ACCEPT_LANGUAGE tells you the natural language preferred by the user—for example, English (en), Danish (dk), or Japanese (jp). You can use this information to make your CGI program sensitive to the language the user understands. This is particularly important on the Internet because users around the world may be trying to understand your program output and error messages.

Getting Input from the Standard Input Stream

The program can read input data from the standard input stream— one long stream of characters—as if typed directly by a user. The program will read the data it needs using typical functions for reading user input from the workstation, a line at a time. This method is preferred when the amount of data cannot be determined ahead of time. This technique is demonstrated in Chapter 6.

Getting Input from the Command Line

The ISINDEX tag is as old as HTML/1.0, but it is still supported and widely used. Web browsers interpret documents with ISINDEX tags by displaying an input area that allows the user to type in a search query. When the user submits the search query by pressing Enter or pushing a special search button, the query string is sent to the Web server, which passes the string on to your CGI program.

41

Each word of the query string becomes an individual command-line argument to your program. Thus, if the user typed "Common Gateway Interface" as the search query, it would be as though they called the CGI program *search.pl* at the command line, as follows:

```
$ search.pl Common Gateway Interface
```

The program usually must then iterate over an array of values to get the various words in the search query.

In Chapter 8, we will construct a simple search gateway program using the ISINDEX tag.

Output from CGI Programs

In terms of output, there are actually two varieties of CGI programs:

- Normal CGI programs, which produce one or more CGI headers, followed by the program output
- NPH programs, which output full HTTP/1.0 response messages. NPH stands for No-Parse Header. With an NPH script, the Web server software doesn't parse or interpret the headers in any way— it just passes them on to the client program.

CGI Headers

Your CGI program must print out special CGI headers before it prints its output. The Web server reads these headers first and then formats the rest of the output into a valid HTTP response to the client program.

We will discuss three common CGI output headers: Content-Type, Location, and Status.

Content-Type

Whenever you return some data to the client program, it must be preceded by the Content-Type header. This header gives the MIME type for the data you are returning, so that it can be properly interpreted by the client program. (See sidebar,"MIME Content Typing.")

Your CGI program needs to output the Content-Type header in the following format:

```
Content-Type: MIME-Content-Type
```

For example

```
Content-Type: text/html
```

This one header will be sufficient for the output of most of your CGI programs.

MIME Content Typing

When a Web server sends a Web resource across the Internet to a client program, the server always includes a *MIME content type.* The MIME standard (Multipurpose Internet Mail Extensions) is adopted from e-mail for attaching nontext files to e-mail messages. The MIME content type tells the client program what kind of resource is being sent (e.g., Video) and its format (e.g., MPEG or QuickTime).

When a Web client program sends form data to a Web server, it also includes a MIME content type for the transmitted data.

Type of Data	MIME Content Type
Text file	text/plain
HTML document	text/html
PostScript document	application/postscript
GIF image	image/gif
JPEG image	image/jpeg
MPEG video	video/mpeg
Contents of an HTML form	application/x-www-form-urlencoded

Location

The Location header gives the URL for the Web resource returned to the client program. It is used frequently to *redirect* the user to a new page without generating an error message. We'll cover this header in more detail in Chapter 7.

Your CGI program needs to output the Location header in the following format:

```
Location: URL
```

For example

```
Location: http://hoohoo.ncsa.uiuc.edu/newhome.html
```

Status

The Status header allows your CGI program to send back status codes to a client to signal an error or provide other data about the CGI program's status.

You can use this header when your CGI program can't generate its intended output, can't access a resource it needs, requires authorization from the user, or encounters some other exception condition. The status code gives the client program the option of retrying, aborting, and so forth. It is good programming practice to use status codes when they are appropriate.

Your CGI program needs to output the following header:

```
Status: Code Reason
```

For example

```
Status: 401 Unauthorized
```

No-Parse Header Programs

All CGI programs with names beginning with "nph-" are No-Parse Header (NPH) programs. These CGI programs must format the full HTTP response message that would normally be composed by your Web server software package.

You can write NPH CGI programs to do things not possible with normal CGI programs. For example, you can write a program that sends its output to the Web browser gradually, instead of all at once. You can use this technique to create moving banners, pages that change every ten seconds, and other tricks. Consult a Web server programming book for details on how to format these headers.

Note: You can also use a programming language such as Java, which runs on the client host machine, to do animations like those described in this section. See *Internet World's 60 Minute Guide to Programming in Java* (IDG Books Worldwide, Inc.).

Performance and Security Concerns with CGI

This section addresses two common concerns about using CGI: the cost to application performance, and the security of the Web site.

Application Performance

The Web server software runs your CGI application programs with a system call, so using a CGI program is often less efficient than compiling your applications directly with the Web server software. Using an Application Program Interface (API), your application's functions will be directly called by Web server code. Many vendors offer server APIs, for example, SpyGlass (SpyGlass ADI) and Netscape (NSAPI). Still, CGI programming is usually preferable to server API programming, as long as the application does not require high performance. In the long run, CGI programs are usually easier to write, install, and test.

Check Chapter 12 for more on server APIs.

Web Site Security Issues

Everyone seems to be interested in Web site security these days—and the risks are real. Should a hacker succeed in breaking into your part of the Internet and run a program on your Web server machine, that program could use up all of your system resources. Your Web services could become unavailable and your server machine could crash. A hacker might also manage to write a program that reads private files containing credit card numbers or passwords.

Such security risks are prevented by special security measures built into Web server software packages:

- To run CGI programs, usually you must be the maintainer of the Web site (Webmaster) or have permission from this person.

- CGI programs must be in a designated place on the server machine, usually the /cgi-bin directory. Programs in other directories cannot be executed by users connecting over the Web.

- Only the Webmaster is permitted to install a Web software package on port 80, the designated port for Web servers. Local area networks often augment security further by putting up *firewalls*—software that prevents users across the Internet from accessing ports other than standard ones.

Passwords and Secure Servers

There are two additional security measures widely available on the Web.

Passwords: The applications programmer can limit access to a particular program by requesting a password from the user. If the password does not match, the Web server will deny access to the application. You have already seen how this is possible using the 401 status code. Chapter 7 gives the programming details.

Secure Servers: You can buy a secure Web server program that will work with a popular Web browser to guarantee secure transmission of sensitive information (credit card numbers, for instance) across the Internet. The browser encrypts the information and transmits the resulting meaningless numbers across the Internet. The secure Web server receives the meaningless numbers and decrypts them back to their original form. Only the browser and the server have the key to properly encrypting and decrypting the messages. Secure Sockets Layer (SSL) is the most popular secure protocol and is supported by most companies, including Netscape and Microsoft.

Even with these sophisticated security techniques available, the Web will never be 100% secure. Before you create CGI programs of your own, be a responsible citizen and learn more about how to make your services secure from intrusion. Chapter 11 provides techniques for making Perl CGI scripts safe from tampering.

What Now?

Now you are familiar with the various ways in which Web server software packages communicate with application programs using CGI. You are also aware of some of the limitations of CGI.

Although you can use the CGI information in this chapter with any programming language, you're about to meet Perl, a popular language for creating CGI programs that is easy to learn. Turn the page and let's get started programming the Web!

## Chapter 3

Perl: A Good Language for CGI Programming

Perl stands for *P*ractical *E*xtraction and *R*eport *L*anguage. It was originally designed for the tasks of extracting information from text files and formatting reports. Today Perl is one of the most popular languages for implementing Internet- and Web-based applications, especially Common Gateway Interface (CGI) programs. People around the world are discovering that Perl is well suited to writing programs for the Internet and the Web.

This chapter is your crash course in Perl. It covers the advantages of using Perl for CGI programming and typical uses for Perl on the Web. It provides an introductory tutorial to the Perl language, with emphasis on features commonly used in CGI programs. When you're done, you'll be prepared to write Perl programs that accomplish everyday programming tasks such as reading user input, searching for patterns in strings, and creating formatted output files. In Part II, we'll apply the techniques you learn here to CGI programming.

Perl on the Web

Why is Perl so popular for CGI programming?

Perl works well for CGI programming because

- Perl is easy to learn. Just a small subset of the language is sufficient to write powerful programs. Perl's overall format is similar to C and to other modern languages. You will be writing real Perl programs in less than an hour!

- Perl supports *scripting,* so programs can be written quickly. You just type your source code into a plain text file and then run this code from a Web browser. (See sidebar, "Why Perl Is a Good Scripting Language.")

- Perl is good at manipulating text files and HTML documents in particular. It offers robust facilities for string processing, pattern matching, and text formatting.

- Perl has a rich set of features for developing CGI applications. Its flexible file input and output routines, access to operating system commands and libraries, and the ability to easily send and receive data over TCP/IP, the most basic Internet protocol, all make Perl ideal for use with CGI.

- Perl also includes support for packaging groups of functions into your own code libraries and modules. Modules are already available for accessing popular database software packages like Oracle 7 and Sybase.

The most recent version of Perl (5.0) has all of the features you've come to expect of modern programming languages, including support for object-oriented programming (OOP).

Perl can be downloaded free from any one of a dozen or so file server machines on the Internet. The language is available for a wide variety of platforms. Perl works well with all major Web server software packages, making it easy to use Perl as the "glue" between your existing applications on your Web server software. In addition, you can utilize the Perl programs in this book to get you started, or access hundreds of programs written by users on the Internet, free of charge.

Why Perl Is a Good Scripting Language

Perl is an ideal scripting language because it has the efficiency of a compiled language and the convenience of an interpreted language.

Your browser runs the Perl source code (script) directly, like an interpreted language. When the script runs, the first thing it does is load the Perl interpreter (**perl**). The interpreter then reads the text of the program and creates an executable, just as a compiled language would do.

Unlike a compiler, **perl** immediately runs the executable version of the program—no binary code stays around on your hard disk. This makes programming Perl less laborious because there is no separate compilation phase. Discounting the time to load the interpreter, Perl programs are often as fast as the equivalent code written in a compiled language such as C. Perl 5.0 includes several performance enhancements that improve execution speed even further.

Scripting greatly accelerates the write/test/debug cycle. You create scripts as small modular units, integrate them into an overall program, and test them with sample data — all without having to write compilation directions and wait for compiles to complete.

Getting Started with Perl

This section explains the available versions of Perl, tells you where to find or download the Perl distribution, and helps you obtain documentation and technical support.

There are two major versions of Perl in use today. Perl 4 has been around longer (it is in patch level 36); Perl 5.0 was recently released.

Note: The examples in this book run under both Perl 4.036 and Perl 5.0 or later, except where otherwise noted.

Finding Out If Perl Is Installed on Your System

If you are on a UNIX platform, you can find out where the **perl** executable is installed by typing the following command:

```
$ which perl
```

If the display from this command is a file system path, such as /usr/local/bin/perl, then you're in business. If you see "perl: not found," then you know that **perl** is not installed at your site.

If **perl** is not installed on your system, you can download it. Follow the instructions in the upcoming section, "Sources for Perl," or ask your system administrator to do it for you.

Finding Out What Version You Have

If **perl** is already installed on your system, then you can find out what version you have by typing the following command. (The dollar sign at the beginning of the line is our command-line prompt.)

```
$ perl -v
```

In response, you'll see something like the following:

```
This is perl, version 5.001

Copyright 1987-1994, Larry Wall

Perl may be copied only under the terms of either the Artistic License
or the GNU General Public License, which may be found in the Perl 5.0
source kit.
```

This indicates you have version 5.0, patch level 1. If you see something like

```
This is perl, version 4.0
```

then you have version 4.

Sources for Perl

Perl is available from a number of sources.

- On Usenet's comp.source.misc or comp.sources.unix archives.
- On Metronet, at

```
http://www.metronet.com/1/perlinfo/source
```

and at a number of other sites on the Web.

- Via Anonymous FTP from *ftp.uu.net* (192.48.96.9).

- Via FTP from UUNET at 1-900-468-7727. Log in as *uucp;* no password is required. Perl is available in the directory ~uucp/gnu. You must pay for this call, so check on rates before starting to download.

- On a CD-ROM included with the book *UNIX Power Tools* by Jerry Peek, Tim O'Reilly, and Mike Loukides (O'Reilly & Associates.)

On-line, you can get a more up-to-date list of Internet sites for downloading **perl.** Look in Tom Christiansen's Perl FAQ, a list of frequently asked questions about Perl. It is available as the first posting to the *comp.lang.perl* Usenet newsgroup. Point your Web browser to *news:comp.lang.perl.* There's a list of Perl archives in the first part of the series, perl-faq/part0.

Platform Availability

Perl is primarily used on the UNIX platform (see sidebar, "Perl's Roots in C and UNIX"), but full-featured versions are available for the Mac (MacPerl), OS/2, Windows 3.1, and Windows NT. A Windows 95 version will probably be out by the time you read this book. See the source archives for specifics on how to download these versions.

Perl's Roots in C and UNIX

Perl was derived from the C language and various UNIX utilities. If you know C, you'll be relieved to find that Perl liberates you from C's pointers, fixed-size data structures, and explicit memory allocation. If you don't know C, don't worry—learning Perl does not require knowledge of C programming.

Perl is a powerful systems programming language. It has all of the capabilities of the **sed** and **awk** UNIX string-processing utilities, and incorporates most functions available in the UNIX shells (**sh, csh,** and **ksh**) but imposes few of their limitations. For example, input lines, arrays, and variable names are allowed to grow as large as the available memory on your system. If you are not familiar with UNIX, you may find Perl's syntax a bit cryptic, but stick with it and you will be rewarded—Perl programs are shorter and thus faster to write than the equivalent code in most other programming languages.

Downloading an Executable Version of Perl

If you are working on a popular operating system version, such as SunOS 4.2, you can download an executable binary form of the Perl interpreter. First download the README file from one of the Perl code archives and look for the exact version of your operating system. Then take the following steps. (In this example, we download a copy of perl 4.036 for Sun OS4.2.1.)

1. Create a directory for the files to download. For instance:

```
$ mkdir /usr/local/pkg/perl4.036
```

2. Point your Web browser to the URL

```
ftp://ftp.uu.net
```

3. Using your browser's file transfer facilities, download the file named /systems/gnu/perl4-036.tar.Z.

4. Since this **perl** file is a .Z tar file, it must be uncompressed and untarred. Enter

```
$ cd /usr/local/pkg/perl4.036
$ cat perl4-036.tar.Z | uncompress | tar xvf -
```

5. The Perl executable is **perl**. You can now move it to a location from which you and other users can access it—/usr/local/bin, for instance.

Caution: You may need special superuser privileges to do this on some systems.

Downloading Source Code

In some system configurations, you will have to download the source files and compile them. You must have a C compiler to do this. Here is an example of how to get Perl 5.0 from *ftp.uu.net*, assuming you will be compiling on a UNIX platform:

1. Create a directory for the files you will download:

```
$ mkdir /usr/local/pkg/perl5.0
```

2. Point your Web browser to the URL

```
ftp://ftp.uu.net
```

3. Select the directory /systems/gnu/perl5.xxx.tar.gz-split.

4. Using your browser, visit files in part1 through partN of this directory and save them to the Perl 5.0 directory that you created in step 1. Save them as part01.tar.gz, part02.tar.gz, and so on.

5. The saved files must be concatenated together, unzipped, and untarred. For example, using the **gunzip** utility, enter

```
$ cd /usr/local/pkg/perl5.0
$ cat *.tar.gz | gunzip | tar xvf -
```

This process extracts a number of files from the tar archive and deposits them in your current directory. To run, follow the instructions in the file named README.

Tip: The **gunzip** utility is available free from *ftp.uu.net*.

---

6. Run the configuration script, compile the source, test the resulting binary, and install the binary. You should install it in a public place, such as /usr/local/bin, if possible.

The compile process for Microsoft Windows is similar, except that you must download and execute a self-extracting archive. Check the instructions in the README file.

Installing Perl 5.0 takes about an hour. The installation requires about 18MB, but the Perl interpreter is only about 0.5MB and you can delete the source code when you are done compiling it.

Getting Perl Documentation

The best and most comprehensive sources of Perl documentation are the following books:

- *Learning Perl* by Randal L. Schwartz (O'Reilly & Associates). A short, gentle introduction to Perl. It covers the language more comprehensively than this chapter does and has a tutorial style.

Perl programmers call this "the Llama book" because a llama figures prominently on its cover.

- *Programming perl* by Larry Wall and Randal L. Schwartz (O'Reilly & Associates). This 465-page reference guide contains a complete description of the language. It is required reading for any serious Perl programmer. Perl programmers call this one "the Camel book."

- *Perl by Example* by Ellie Quigley (Prentice Hall, 1995). This one is a good source of short Perl examples. It includes sections on advanced topics such as interprocess communication. We dub this "the Examples book," since it sports no four-legged creature on the cover.

In addition, Tom Christiansen's Perl FAQ on Usenet, mentioned earlier in this chapter, contains answers to frequently asked questions.

Tip: On UNIX systems, you can enter the command $man perl to display the on-line manual page. This documentation is fairly dense, so you may prefer to start with the other sources listed in this section.

Getting Technical Support

No single software company supports Perl; nor does it have a toll-free technical support line. However, the *comp.lang.perl* Usenet newsgroup mentioned earlier provides a forum for getting answers to tough Perl questions. If you want to join the mailing list, you can send e-mail to

```
perl-users-request@virginia.edu
```

Not surprisingly, support from the Perl extended on-line family is often faster, of higher quality, and certainly cheaper than support from a hotline. Larry Wall, the inventor of Perl, will often answer difficult questions on *comp.lang.perl,* and if you have a hard question you can even e-mail him directly at NetLabs.

You'll also find bug reports and patches to the **perl** executable, posted to *comp.lang.perl.* Each patch comes with installation instructions that are easy to follow.

See Chapter 13 for more sources of technical support.

An Introduction to Perl

The remainder of this chapter gives a quick overview of Perl for those of you already familiar with programming concepts. If you need an in-depth tutorial, try the *Learning Perl* book referenced earlier. The introduction given here is not comprehensive, but it will give you enough familiarity with Perl to understand the CGI programs in this book and create similar programs on your own.

Here, you'll start by learning how to assign values to variables, read from and write to files, test variables for when certain conditions become true, look for complex patterns in strings of characters, and repeat blocks of code. You'll also see how to modularize your programs using functions, packages, and libraries. Finally, we'll give a brief over-view of object-oriented programming in Perl 5.0. Using these techniques, you will be able to create most of the CGI code that you will need.

Writing Your First Perl Program

A Perl program is simply a sequence of Perl *statements*. The usual way to create a Perl program is to create a script by putting these statements into a text file. Follow these steps:

1. Create a text file using your favorite editor.
   a. In UNIX this is usually either **vi** or **emacs**.
   b. In Windows 3.1 you can use the Notepad program.
      Or, if you use Microsoft Word or another word
      processor, be sure to save the file as plain ASCII text.

2. Add some Perl statements, one to a line, ending each line with a semicolon. Perl statements are usually in the form

```
operator(arg1, arg2, ..., argN)
```

   For example, you might add this statement:

```
print("Hello World!\n");
```

   This **print** statement sends a character string to standard output, which goes to your monitor. Be sure to add the \n before ending the string you want printed; this adds a newline character.

55

The newline is equivalent to the user pressing Enter.

3. When you've finished adding statements, add any needed comments. Comments start with a pound sign (#) and continue to the end of a line. Here, we've added a comment after the **print** statement:

```
print("Hello World!\n"); # Print this line to standard output.
```

4. Name the file and save it. There is no standard file-naming convention for Perl programs, but the most prevalent way to name files is to add the extension .pl, making our program name hello.pl.

That's it! You don't have to create a project file, compile the program, or add a main routine. Your program is ready to run.

Running Your Program

The easiest way to run your Perl program is to run the Perl interpreter, **perl**, from a command line. For our file hello.pl, you would type the following:

```
$ perl hello.pl
```

to get this on your screen

```
Hello World!
```

If you want to be able to run Perl programs from an icon in a windowing environment, or as a script from a command line, take the steps outlined in the following sections.

Running Perl Programs from Icons

If you are running Microsoft Windows or some other windowing environment, you may want to create an icon that will run your Perl program. In Windows 3.1, follow the Program Manager's Help information to create a Program Item icon. Then do the following:

1. Choose an icon for your program, and then select File|Properties in the Program Manager. You should see the Program Item Properties dialog.

2. In the Command Line field, enter the exact command line to execute your program, as if you were typing into DOS. For our system, Perl 5.0 is installed in the perl5 directory on the C drive, so we would enter the following:

```
C:\perl5\perl hello.pl
```

After you have created an icon for your program, you can double-click on that icon to start it running.

Running Perl Programs as Scripts

When writing CGI programs, you will want to turn your Perl programs into scripts. If you are using a UNIX command shell (**sh, ksh,** or **csh,** for instance), you can convert a Perl source code file into an executable script by inserting the command to run **perl** directly into your Perl source code. Do this:

1. Place the following commented Perl script header line at the top of your source code file on a line by itself:

```
#!/usr/local/bin/perl
```

2. Save the source code file.
3. Make the file executable from a command line, if necessary. For our file named hello.pl, you would type the following at the UNIX prompt:

```
$ chmod +x hello.pl
```

Our program is now an executable script. Here is our hello.pl program:

```
#!/usr/local/bin/perl
# Hello.pl
print("Hello World!\n");  # Print this line to standard output.
```

To run the program, you just type the name of the file at a command line:

```
$ hello.pl
```

Or, if you are not in the directory where the program resides, you'll need to enter the complete directory path:

```
$ /etc/httpd/cgi-bin/hello.pl
```

Tip: As a shortcut, you can add the program directory /etc/httpd/cgi-bin onto the end of your executable search path (*PATH* variable). Then type hello.pl.

Working with Character Strings

Like most programming languages, Perl lets you assign and later use variables. Most variables that you will manipulate in Perl will be character strings. You can assign these strings to variables and then use special formatting conventions to generate your output.

Variable Assignment

Assigning variables is easy in Perl. Here's how to assign the Internet domain name for the White House Web server to the variable *$server:*

```
$server = 'www.whitehouse.gov';
```

Note: When assigning variables, use descriptive names whenever possible. Perl puts no limit on the length of a variable name.

In most compiled languages, including C, you have to declare each variable before you use it in your code. In Perl, there are no variable declarations, so a variable like *$server* in our example can be assigned a value without declaring it to be a string of characters.

You can assign strings to much longer sequences of characters, too, such as the contents of a Web server log file or an HTML document. Perl has no built-in limits on the size of strings; it allocates memory for string variables as needed. Though we wouldn't recommend it, you can keep right on adding characters to a string until all of the available memory on your machine is exhausted!

You may notice that there are no functions for reading and writing numbers to data files. Perl automatically converts all numbers to strings if the operator requires a string argument, so you can just do

58

numeric calculations and then manipulate the result as a string value. This comes in very handy when dealing with HTML forms that include text fields where the user inputs numbers.

String Formatting

Strings come in two varieties: single-quoted (as in 'Internet') and double-quoted (as in "Internet\n"). The main difference between the two is that double-quoted strings can include special *backslashed characters* that control formatting. Examples of these are \n (newline), \t (tab), and \u (uppercase next letter).

The following program:

```
print("The World-Wide Web\nThe Internet\n");
```

prints out two phrases on two different lines:

```
The World-Wide Web
The Internet
```

Note: In Perl 5.0, the **uc** operator will convert a string to uppercase; the **lc** operator will convert it to lowercase.

Variable Interpolation

Perl also substitutes for variables that occur inside double-quoted strings, so the following program:

```
$server = 'www.whitehouse.gov';
print("The Net address is $server\n");
```

prints out this line:

```
The Net address is www.whitehouse.gov
```

Accessing Files

Perl makes it easy to read from and write to files using *filehandles*. These filehandles are simply names of places to send and receive a stream of data. Perl provides several predefined filehandles for standard input and output to the terminal, plus you can define your own filehandles for reading and writing data files from other sources, including your disk drives.

Using Predefined Filehandles

You can read a line of input (up to the first newline character) with a statement like the following:

```
$server = <STDIN>;
```

In this example, when we assign the STDIN filehandle to a variable, we get a line of input from the terminal. Wrapping a filehandle in brackets (< and >) is a shortcut for reading in data. Each time you assign <STDIN> to a variable, you will get another line of input.

If you want to read a specific number of characters, use the **read** function.

Here is a complete list of Perl's built-in filehandles:

FILEHANDLE	PURPOSE
STDIN	Reading standard input from the terminal
STDOUT	Writing standard output to the terminal
STDERR	Writing error output to the terminal
ARGV	Reading arguments from the command line

The **print** operator always outputs to STDOUT when you do not specify a filehandle as an argument. If you want to print to error output, for instance, you must use the following STDERR filehandle, as in the statement:

```
print(STDERR,"Sorry, that is not a valid URL.\n");
```

Note: It isn't necessary to include the parentheses with many of Perl's operators. For example, the statement

```
print STDERR "Bad URL\n"
```

is equivalent to

```
print(STDERR, "Bad URL\n")
```

Extracting a Subset of a String

Perl does not automatically drop the newline character when it reads from a file. The string operator **chop** removes the last character from a string, so it is often used to chop off a newline just after a line is read in, like this:

```
$server = <STDIN>;  # read a line
chop $server;        # chop off the newline
print "The Web server $server is up\n";
```

The **chop** operator has the side effect of assigning a new value to its argument, in this case *$server.*

You can usually ignore the return value of **chop** because Perl just returns the character that was chopped. If you really want to extract one or more characters from a string, you can use **substr**:

- **substr**(*string, offset*) returns the substring of *string* starting at *offset.* The *offset* starts at zero. If it is negative, **substr** will count from the end of the string, so **substr**(*string*, -1) is equivalent to **chop**(*string*).

Putting User-Defined Filehandles to Work

When you want to create your own I/O channels to files, you define your own filehandles. In this section we'll look at how to accomplish reading and writing from user-defined filehandles, and then how to close these filehandles when you are done with them.

Reading Your Input from a File

Reading input from a user-defined filehandle is similar to reading input from standard input, except that you must first use **open** to name the filehandle.

Tip: When using predefined filehandles or defining your own, use all UPPERCASE letters.

The following code opens the file named access.log, reads in a line at a time using a filehandle named LOG, and prints out each line to standard output with a prefix:

```
open(LOG, 'access.log');
while (<LOG>) {
    chop; # remove from next line in log file
    print "Accessed host: $_.\n";
}
```

Whenever you read a line of input from a filehandle, Perl automatically assigns the input line to the predefined *default pattern matching variable* $_. This variable is also the default value for most operators that take character strings as arguments (see sidebar, "Default Values for Optional Arguments").

Default Values for Optional Arguments

Some arguments to Perl operators are optional—if you don't specify them, Perl will provide default values for you. For example, if you omit the second argument of **print** or the only argument to **chop**, Perl fills in the value of the default pattern matching variable. Filehandle arguments are often optional and default to a predefined filehandle, such as STDIN, STDOUT, or ARGV. Chapter 4 of the Camel book lists each Perl operator, its required and optional arguments, and any default values.

Writing Your Output to a File

To open a file for writing, change the filename to > *file*. To append to the end of a file, use >> *file*. For example, to log output to /tmp/log, use this statement:

```
open(FILE, '> /tmp/log')
```

If a required file cannot be opened for output, you can print an error message to the standard error output, using the **die** operator:

```
open(FILE, '> /tmp/log') || die("Couldn't create /tmp/log\n");
```

Here the two vertical bars (||) specify a logical disjunction, so if the file cannot be opened, the **die** operator will print an error message with the line number, and terminate the program.

Closing Files

When you are done with a file, it is good practice to **close** it:

```
close(LOG);
```

If you don't close a file, Perl will close it for you when your program exits. See Table 3-1 for a list of useful filehandle operators.

Table 3-1: Useful Filehandle Operators

OPERATOR	PURPOSE
open(FILEHANDLE,"*filename*")	Opens a file
close(FILEHANDLE)	Closes a file
die(STRING)	Prints STRING to STDERR and exits the program
eof(FILEHANDLE)	Returns 1 if the next read will return end-of-file
print(FILEHANDLE, STRING)	Prints a string to FILEHANDLE

Branching Execution

Branching (conditional) execution in Perl is done using either the **if** statement or the **unless** statement. Tests are done with comparison operators. There are separate sets of operators for strings and numbers.

The If Statement

Perl has an **if** statement much like that employed in other languages. It does a test and, if the test is successful (that is, it results in a nonempty string), a block of statements (enclosed in curly braces) is executed.

Unlike C, the curly braces are always required for blocked statements:

```
if ($name eq 'Webmaster') {
   print "Welcome, Webmaster.\n";
} elsif ($name eq 'root') {
   print "Welcome, superuser.\n";
} else {
   print "Welcome, user!\n";
}
```

Note that you must use **elsif**, not **elseif** or **elif**.

63

The Unless Statement

When the conditional test fails rather than succeeds, the **unless** statement executes the statements that follow, as shown in the following example:

```
unless ($server eq 'www.whitehouse.com') {
    print "Cannot run on $server. Try www.whitehouse.com\n";
}
```

This script prints a warning message when $server is not www.whitehouse.com. Otherwise, it proceeds to the next statement.

There is no **case** or **switch** statement in Perl; you must use the **if** statement instead.

Comparison Operators

Perl has two different classes of comparison operators; one for comparing strings and one for numbers—and you must use the correct one. For example:

- When comparing two strings for equivalence, use **eq**. It returns 1 (true) if both strings are identical (for example, *$month* **eq** "Dec").

- When comparing two numbers for equivalence, use the double equals sign (==). It returns 1 (true) if they are numerically the same (for example, *$month* == 12).

Both classes of operators return 1 as a true value and the empty string (' ') as a false value. Zero in a string form ("0") also counts as a false value. Common comparison operators of each type are listed in Table 3-2.

Table 3-2: Useful Comparison Operators

TYPE OF COMPARISON	NUMERIC OPERATOR	STRING OPERATOR
Equal to	==	eq
Less than	<	lt
Greater than	>	gt
Less than or equal to	<=	le
Greater than or equal to	>=	ge
Not equal to	!=	ne

Caution: Strings are compared character by character, not as numbers. So '45' comes before '9' because the first character in the first string ('4') has a lower ASCII value than the first character in the second string ('9').

Useful Operators for String Comparisons

Perl provides several operators that come in handy when doing string comparisons.

In addition to **chop**, which we already discussed, the following functions are available:

- **length**(*string*) returns the number of characters in *string*.

- **index**(*string, substring*) returns the position of the first occurrence of *substring* in *string*.

- **rindex**(*string, substring*) returns the position of the last occurrence of *substring* in *string*.

Searching and Substituting

If you want to do more than just simple comparisons between strings, you will need to use Perl's pattern-matching operators. With these operators you can search for patterns and substitute for matched strings.

Searching for Patterns with the Match Operator

Perl's match operator is /*pattern*/. This operator will search for a certain *pattern* in a string of characters—say, a particular word in a text file. When you use an operator with its proper arguments and it returns a value, it is called an *expression*.

Note: The match operator is really **m**/*pattern*/ where the **m** stands for *match*, but the **m** is optional and rarely used.

For example, to search for the string *gov,* you would use the expression

```
/gov/
```

Matching to the Default Pattern-Matching Variable

Perl matches the sequence of characters in the pattern to the default pattern-matching variable, $_. If the pattern is found, the program returns true; otherwise, false. Thus, the following code

```
print "Please enter URLs, one to a line.\n";
while (<STDIN>) {
   if (/gov/) {
      print "$_ is a government Web site.\n";
   }
}
```

will read input from the terminal and print a message if the characters that you input contain the substring *gov*.

If you type in the following URL

```
http://www.whitehouse.gov/index.html
```

it will match the pattern and the program will print

```
http://www.whitehouse.gov is a government Web site.
```

If you instead type

```
www.whitehouse.office
```

it will not match the pattern and hence nothing would be printed.

Ignoring Case in the Match

You can make the match insensitive to the case of the pattern by putting an **i** switch after the match operator, as follows:

```
if (/gov/i) {
   print "$_ is a government Web site.\n";
}
```

Matching to a Different String

To match a string other than $_, you must use the =~ operator. For example, here is some code to search for the string, gov, in the string variable $url:

```
if ($url =~ /gov/) {
   print "$url is a government Web site.\n";
}
```

Using Regular Expressions

To look for a special type of pattern, such as a line starting with a word and ending with a number, you will need to use *regular expressions*. Regular expressions are just strings with special characters that specify particular ways of matching to the input string.

Using Special Characters for Matching

You can specify that a given character in a string should be a digit (**\d**), an alphanumeric character (**\w**), or a space (**\s**). For example, suppose the variable *$address* is set to a mailing address. You can use the match operator with special characters to test whether this address includes three digits (the house number), a space, and four alphanumeric characters (the street name).

```
if ($address =~ /\d\d\d\s\w\w\w\w/) {
    print "Mail address is in correct format\n";
}
```

This pattern would match and the message would be printed if you assigned *$address* as follows:

```
$address = '444 Hoes Lane';
```

but not if you assigned it as

```
$address = '44 Hoes Lane';
```

Skipping Single Characters

Particular characters can be skipped using the dot (.), which matches any single character except a newline. For example, to accept any character (not just a space) between the house number and street, use the expression

```
/\d\d\d.\w\w\w\w/   # match 3 digits, any one char,  4 word chars
```

This pattern would now match if *$address* were assigned as follows:

```
$address = 444-Rand St;
```

Matching Multiple Occurrences

An asterisk (*) will match zero or more occurrences of a character, so the expression \s* will skip over any number of spaces (including none). For example, this next expression matches a house number consisting of any number of digits, followed by any number of spaces, followed by any number of alphanumeric characters:

```
/\d*\s*\w*/    # match to digits, zero or more spaces, then a word.
```

You can also search for one or more occurrences of a character using plus sign (+) and zero or one occurrences using a question mark (?).

Anchoring Your Pattern

You may want to *anchor* your pattern instead of allowing it to match anywhere in the string. The carat (^) matches the beginning of a string; the dollar sign ($) matches the end of a string. For example, the following expression matches a line that starts with a house number and ends with the character string "St.":

```
/^\d+\s+\w*St\.$/
```

Notice that the period just before $/ is preceded by a backslash; this is necessary to keep it from being interpreted as the dot (.) pattern-matching character. You must add a blackslash before all special characters if you want to find them in a string, including forward slash (/), question mark (?), asterisk (*), plus sign (+), and dollar sign ($).

Including Variables in Your Pattern

You can include variables in your strings. In the special case where the dollar sign ($) is at the end of a string, it is interpreted as a special pattern-matching character instead of as the beginning of a variable.

Remembering Matched Substrings

If you need to extract a substring from a longer string, you can use parentheses to delimit the part of the pattern that you want to find and remember. For example, here's how to extract just the street name and then print it out:

```
if ($address =~ /^\d+\s+(\w*)St\.$/) {
    print "You live on $1.\n";
}
```

If *$address* is assigned as follows

```
$address = "444 Dunmore St.";
```

then this code would print out

```
You live on Dunmore.
```

Each time a substring is remembered using parentheses, it is stored in a different variable (*$1, $2, $3,* and so on).

Substituting for Matched Strings

When you want to substitute a new string for the part of a string that matched a pattern, use the substitute operator, *s/old/new.* For example, the following code will substitute *ftp* for *http* in all input lines:

```
while (<STDIN>) {
   if (s/http/ftp/) {
      print;
      }
   }
```

Substituting for All Occurrences

When you want to substitute for all occurrences of a pattern on a line, rather than just the first occurrence, add a **g** after the slash following the *new* string:

```
s/http/ftp/g
```

Perl does the substitution using the default pattern-matching variable $_.

Assigning the Result of the Substitution

You can assign the result of a substitution to a new variable, using the =~ operator. For example

```
$url = "http://whitehouse.gov";
$ftpurl =~ s/http/ftp/;
print "The ftp URL is: $ftpurl.\n";
```

This code will print the string

```
ftp://whitehouse.gov
```

Repeating Blocks of Code

Perl has three types of loops for repeating blocks of code: the **while** loop, the **until** loop, and the **foreach** loop. The **foreach** loop is covered in the next section on arrays.

The While Loop

The **while** loop is similar to C's **while** loop. This example adds an HTML list-item tag to the start of each input line:

```
while (<STDIN>) {
  chop;
  print "<LI> $_.\n";
}
```

The Until Loop

The **until** loop is identical to the **while** loop, except that the **until** loop tests whether the expression is false instead of whether it is true. The following **until** loop reads and prints each line until it reaches the end of file, at which point it prints an error message and exits:

```
$error = 0;
until ($error) {
   if ($_ = <STDIN>){
      chop;
      print "Read: $_\n";
   }
   else {
      print "End of file!\n";
      $error = 1;
   }
}
```

Using Arrays

Perl provides two types of arrays: *simple arrays* and *associative arrays*. Simple arrays hold a list of values. Associative arrays hold a list of keys with their corresponding values.

Simple Arrays

Perl arrays hold a sequence of numbers or strings. The @ designates a simple array variable. Like most data structures in Perl, an array can have any number of elements. Here we will set the array variable *@url* to a list of three things: a domain name, a port, and a path to a resource:

```
@url = ("www.whitehouse.gov:", 80, "/usr/bill/bosnia/solution");
```

Arrays are indexed by numbers starting at zero, so they can be subscripted to get individual elements, as in C. For example, *@url[2]* is *"/usr/bill/bosnia/solution"*.

Here is an example where we concatenate and print the first and last elements of the *@url* array variable:

```
@url = ("www.whitehouse.gov:", 80, "/usr/bill/bosnia/solution");
print $url[0] . $url[2];
```

The output of this code is

```
www.whitehouse.gov/usr/bill/bosnia/solution
```

See Table 3-3 for a list of useful array operators.

Table 3-3: Useful Array Operators

OPERATOR	PURPOSE
shift(*@array*)	Removes the first element of *@array*
unshift(*@array, $new*)	Adds *$new* to the front of *@array*
pop(*@array*)	Removes the last element of *@array* and returns it
push(*@array,$new*)	Adds *$new* as the last element of *@array*
split(/*pattern*/, *$line*)	Matches *pattern* to *$line,* to split it into substrings; returns an array of these substrings.
join(*$glue, @arraylist*)	The opposite of split. Puts together a string consisting of the elements of *@arraylist,* with *$glue* in between
sort(*@array*)	Sorts strings in ASCII order

The **split** and **join** operators in Table 3-3 are useful for breaking apart directory paths and URLs and putting them back together again.

The Foreach Loop

Perl also provides a **foreach** statement for easily looping over an array. This example loops over the elements in the *@hostlog* array variable:

```
open(FILE, "host.log") || die "Cannot open host log file!";
@hostlog = <FILE>;
foreach $host (@hostlog) {
   chop $host;
   print "You had a visit from $host.\n";
}
```

Associative Arrays

An associative array is a collection of key-value pairs. Given a key, the associative array returns the corresponding value. The keys and values can be strings, so you can make arbitrary links between character string data in your program.

Associative array variables are preceded by a percent sign (%). The following code assigns a set of initial keys and values to an associative array variable called *%userdata*:

```
%userdata = (
   'domain', 'idgbooks.com',
   'port', 80,
   );
```

In Perl 5.0, you should use the new attribute reference operator (=>) when defining associative arrays:

```
%userdata = (
   'domain' => 'idgbooks.com',
   'port' => 80,
   );
```

The following code assigns a value of 'idgbooks.com' to the key 'domain' in the associative array *%userdata:*

```
$userdata{'domain'} = 'idgbooks.com';
```

Here the expression *$userdata{'domain'}* is an *array variable reference.* The string 'domain' now *points to* 'idgbooks.com'. To retrieve and print the value of *domain* use the statement

```
print "The machine is $userdata{'domain'}";
```

Note: When we are dealing with individual elements of simple arrays or assciative arrays, the array variable reference begins with a dollar sign ($) as if it was a normal string variable.

See Table 3-4 for a list of useful associative array operators.

Table 3-4: Useful Associative Array Operators

ARRAY OPERATOR	PURPOSE
keys(%array)	Returns an array of all of the keys of %array without the values and in no guaranteed order
values(%array)	Returns an array of all the values of %array without the keys
each(%array)	Allows you to step through an associative array, one key-value pair at a time

A common technique is to iterate over the keys, printing values. Here is a program using the **each** array operator. It prints each key and value in the associative array *%userdata:*

```
while (($key,$value) = each(%userdata)) {
    print "$key is $value\n";
```

In this example, **each** returns an array of two values: the key and its corresponding value. When there are no more pairs, **each** returns the empty string and the **while** loop exits.

Modularizing Your Programs

Perl provides modern language features for *modularizing* your programs and providing *abstractions.* You can create functions, variables local to those functions, packages for encapsulating functions and variables, and libraries to hold programs in a separate source file.

Names in Perl

The Perl language employs lots of different types of names: names for variables that hold strings and numbers ($x), arrays (@x), associative arrays (%x), as well as functions (&x), labels (x), and filehandles (x). You can use the same name for each of these elements without fear of confusion because each is a separate name to **perl**. Nevertheless, we recommend that you *not* use the same name for two different variables, subroutines, or labels.

Functions

In this section, we explain how to define and call functions that take arguments and return values.

Defining Functions

Use the **sub** command to define a function, as shown here:

```
sub print_header {
    print "Content-type: text/html\n\n";
}
```

This function has no parameters and no return value.

Note: The **sub** is short for *subroutine*. In Perl, functions are often called subroutines, even if they take parameters and return a value.

Calling Functions

After you've defined a function, you can call it by preceding its name with an ampersand (&). For example, we can call the *print_header* function in a script as follows:

```
#!/usr/local/bin/perl
&print_header;
print "This is an HTML document.\n";
```

Note: You should place all of your functions at the end of the program file.

Returning a Value from a Function

To have a function return a value back to its calling routine or the main program, use the **return** statement:

```
sub get_header {
return("Content-type: text/html\n\n");
    }
```

You can use the value returned from a function in any Perl expression:

```
print &get_header();
```

If there are no arguments to the function, you can omit the parentheses:

```
print &get_header;
```

Using Local Variables in Functions

Variables in Perl are always global unless you declare them to be local. You do this using the **local** operator, as follows:

```
sub get_header {
    local($mime_type, $mime_subtype);
    $mime_type = 'text';
    $mime_subtype = 'html';
    return("Content-type: $mime_type/$mime_subtype\n\n");
}
```

A **local** statement makes a variable (or a list of variables) visible only within the enclosing function. In our example, both *$mime_subtype* and *$mime_type* will have undefined values outside of the *get_header* function.

Initializing Local Variables

You can a declare set of local variables and initialize them in one step, as this version of our get_header function demonstrates:

```
sub get_header {
    local($mime_type, $mime_subtype) = ('text', 'html');
    return("Content-type: $mime_type/$mime_subtype\n\n");
}
```

Specifying Parameters to Functions

In Perl, you can pass any number of arguments to a function. When you call a function, the argument list is automatically set to the pre-defined local array variable, @_. Although you can access this array using $_[0], $_[1], and so on, nobody does this. Instead, @_ is assigned to an array of local variables (the *parameters*) in the first statement of the function.

Here is an improved version of our get_header function with *$mime_type* and *$mime_subtype* as parameters:

```
# Returns the correct CGI header for the MIME type and subtype
sub get_header {
    local($mime_type, $mime_subtype) = @_;
    return("Content-type: $mime_type/$mime_subtype\n\n");
}
```

Now the call to our get_header function becomes

```
print &get_header('text', 'html');
```

Tip: Get in the habit of carefully commenting all parameters and return values.

Packages

If you want to use a variable in more than one function, but not have it be accessible globally, you can use a *package*. A package is designated by adding a **package** declaration at the top of a file or before a block of statements. Let's call our *get_headers* function, but hide it in a package:

```
print &Header'get_header('text', 'html');
```

This is a *package reference*. In Perl 5.0, you can create a package reference using a double colon (::) as follows:

```
print &Header::get_header('text', 'html');
```

In this same file, you should define the package. For example:

```
package Header; # define a package called Header
sub get_header {    # This function is now in this package
```

```
    local($mime_type, $mime_subtype) = @_;
    return("Content-type: $mime_type/$mime_subtype\n\n");
}
```

Libraries

Perl comes with a standard library, for useful, predefined functions call the Standard Perl Library. You can also create libraries of your own that you can use in your programs or distribute to other Perl users.

The Standard Perl Library

In order to use functions from the Standard Perl Library in your Perl programs, you must first **require** the library file that includes the function or functions you want to use.

Let's take a look at how to use a function from a library. The standard library contains a file, ctime.pl, that includes a function **ctime** for printing out a human-readable date (and time). To call the **ctime** function in our code, we must first **require** the ctime.pl library file:

```
require 'ctime.pl';
```

and use it as follows:

```
print &ctime(time);
```

This code outputs something like the following:

```
Fri Oct  6 22:29:22 US/Eastern 1995
```

User-Defined Libraries

You can collect a set of functions in your own library file. These libraries can be included by other users in their code, using the **require** command. For example, if we put our *get_header* function in a separate file named header-lib.pl (most libraries end in *lib*), another programmer could use the functions in this library as follows:

```
#!/usr/local/bin/perl5
# This script prints a simple HTML document.
require 'header-lib.pl';
print &Header::get_header('text', 'html');
print "This is an HTML document.\n";
```

> **Tip:** Users who **require** your library may need to add a library file directory to the pre-defined array @*INC* as follows: `push(@INC,"/etc/httpd/cgi-bin")`; This statement should be inserted at the top of the program file, before any **require** statements.

Object-Oriented Programming in Perl 5.0

Perl 5.0 includes a number of features to support object-oriented programming (OOP), including functions for creating objects, getting and setting attributes of objects, defining and calling methods, and nesting definitions of objects one inside the other. For details on using inheritance and other advanced features, see the Perl 5.0 Web page at

```
http://www.metronet.com/perlinfo/perl5.html
```

Creating Objects

Objects are either *classes* (types) or *instances* (examples). In Perl 5.0, you define a new object class every time you create a package. New instances of this class can be defined using the **bless** operator within that package. For example, the following code creates a new instance of the class named Mime:

```
package Mime;
$obj1 = bless {'type' => 'text', 'subtype' => 'html'};
```

Now *$obj1* is an object instance of type Mime. It has two attributes: *type* and *subtype*. The single argument to **bless** in curly braces is an example of an *anonymous object definition*. It is really just a fancy way of designating an associative array that doesn't yet have a name. The variable *$obj1* simply provides a reference (pointer) to the object instance so that we can retrieve values from its attributes.

Getting Attributes of Objects

To get the value of an attribute, use the *object reference operator* (->). For example, to print the value of the 'type' attribute of the anonymous object assigned to *$obj1,* do the following:

```
print $obj1->{'type'};
```

To print the MIME content type, do the following:

```
print $obj1->{'type'} . '/' . $obj1->{'subtype'};
```

Remember, the dot operator (.) concatenates two strings, so this produces a legal MIME content type string like the following:

```
text/html
```

Setting Attributes of Objects

You can also use the object reference operator to set values of attributes. For example, this sets the value of 'type' to 'text':

```
$obj1->{'type'} = 'text';
```

Defining Methods

Functions that apply to a given object class are called *methods*. Usually you will want to define a *constructor method* for creating an instance of a given object class and several *access methods* and *set methods* to get and put attribute values, respectively.

In this example, we define a *new* method to create an instance of the Mime class, and get_type and get_subtype methods to get the two different attributes of a Mime object:

```
package Mime;
# Creates a new instance of a Mime object.
sub new {
   return bless {}; # you must include these curly braces
}
sub get_type {
   local($object) = @_;
   return $object->{'type'};
}
sub get_subtype {
   local($object) = @_;
   return $object->{'subtype'};
}
```

Calling Methods

After you have defined a set of methods for an object class, such as Mime, you can call these methods using the object reference operator (→). For example, this calls the *get_type* and *get_subtype* methods:

```
sub get_format {
    local($object) = @_;
    return($object->get_type() . '/' . $object->get_subtype());
}
```

If you want to call a method from outside of a package, you can use the package reference (::) we introduced earlier. Here we call the constructor method for the Mime object class to create a new instance:

```
$obj1 = &Mime::new;
```

This is equivalent to calling **bless** directly, except this code doesn't have to be placed in the Mime package.

After we have a reference to an object instance, such as $obj1, we can call this object's methods using the object reference operator (→), even if the code we are writing is not enclosed in the same package. For example, we can use *get_format* method in the Mime class as follows:

```
sub get_header {
    local($object) = @_;
    return('Content-type: ' . $object->get_format() . "\n\n");
}
```

We can now call *get_header* with the reference to the Mime object instance that we would like to use ($obj1 in this example), :

```
print &get_header($obj1);
```

Here we have *encapsulated* the details of the Mime format within the Mime object class, hiding the specifics from the calling function. This makes it much easier to create larger and more modular programs.

Nesting Object Definitions

In Perl 5.0, you can nest objects, one inside the other:

```
$mime_types = bless { 'hypertext' => { 'type'    => 'text',
                                        'subtype' => 'html' }
                    };
```

This defines an anonymous object, *$mime_types,* with one attribute: 'hypertext'. The value of this attribute is another anonymous object definition:

```
{ 'type' => 'text',
  'subtype' => 'html' }
```

Thus, to print the 'subtype' attribute of the *$mime_types* object, we could do the following:

```
print $mime_types->{'hypertext'}->{'subtype'};
```

This will display

```
html
```

Moving On to Part II

This ends our crash course on Perl. In the next chapter, you will see how to write CGI programs that utilize the Perl features you've learned so far.

Part **Two**

CGI Scripting in Perl

In this part, you'll study Perl's role in programming CGI scripts. You'll find out how to

- Create your own CGI scripts — and fix them when they break
- Move your CGI scripts without causing headaches for people visiting your Web site
- Create Web pages with dynamic content
- Use a Web browser to check the time, compose and send e-mail, and more
- Create and process forms
- Add cool search capabilities to your Web site

Let's get started.

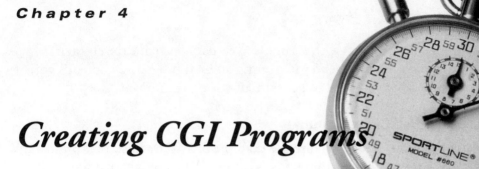

## Chapter 4

Creating CGI Programs

C ommon Gateway Interface (CGI) programming enables you to take advantage of the power of the World-Wide Web. Using CGI, you can create programs that users can run from across the Internet, using just a standard Web browser. These *CGI scripts,* also known as *CGIs* or *gateway scripts,* can add a new level of interactivity to your Web pages.

This chapter describes how to write basic CGI programs using Perl. We will go through the process of developing — including writing, testing, and debugging — a simple interactive Web page that uses a CGI script. In the process, you'll learn how to

- Create CGI scripts in Perl using an easy six-step process
- Catch errors *before* you make your CGI script available to other users
- Use **perl** and Web server error messages to inform your debugging
- Install your program on a Web server machine
- Trace the execution of your CGI programs

    Let's get started!

Developing CGI Programs

This section starts with a sample Web page, explains the six-step process we recommend for creating all CGI programs, and ends with a list of what you need to get started writing your own CGIs.

The Web Clock Example

In this chapter we will use the example of a Web Clock that prints out the current time whenever you visit its URL. You will first write a program that displays the current time to the Web browser. You will then create a Web Clock home page (see Figure 4-1) that provides a way for users to run this program.

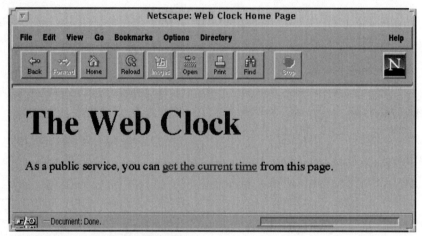

Figure 4-1: The Web Clock home page.

Notice in Figure 4-1 the hyperlink "get the current time." When the user clicks on this, the resulting output will look like that displayed in Figure 4-2. This *dynamic Web page,* titled "Web Clock Output," is generated by a CGI program rather than created in an editor.

Six Easy Steps to Creating a CGI Program

We recommend that you follow these six steps when creating CGI programs:

1. Write the program.
2. Test the program alone.

3. Move the program to a CGI script directory.

4. Run the program as a CGI script from your Web browser.

5. Fix any errors or problems with the output.

6. Create a Web page that lets the user conveniently access your CGI program.

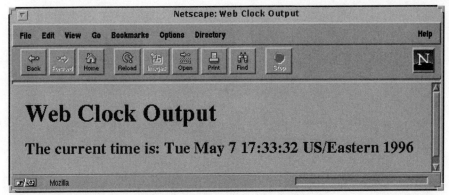

Figure 4-2: This Web Clock Output page is the result of clicking on a hyperlink on the Web Clock home page.

The remainder of this chapter illustrates these six steps using the Web Clock example.

Tools You'll Need Before Getting Started

To start writing CGI programs, you will need access to the following software:

- Perl version 4.036 or 5.0. We used Perl 5.001 for this book.

- A CGI/1.1-compliant Web server software package. We used NCSA HTTPd 1.4.1.

- An HTML/2.0-compliant Web browser. We used Netscape Navigator 1.1.

Many of the examples in this book, including the Web Clock, are available at `http://www.idgbooks.com/idgbooksonline/CGI`.

The project you'll work on in this chapter is devised for an arrangement in which Perl, the Web browser, and the Web server software are all running on the same "development" machine. Ultimately, you will want to test your CGI programs from a Web browser running on a different machine that is connected to your development machine via the Internet.

As you work through the rest of Part II, you will need to know the basics of HTML. There are a number of good books available on HTML, including *HTML for Dummies* (1995), from IDG Books Worldwide, Inc.

Writing the Program

For a CGI program using Perl, you create a standard Perl program, except that you must do the following:

- Print the CGI headers as your first line of output
- Print a document title
- Print out the document body using HTML codes

Printing the CGI Header

The CGI headers tell your Web server software package about the information you are returning from your CGI program. Most of the time you will be returning an HTML document to the user, so you will have to start your program with the Content-Type CGI header, as follows:

```
#!/usr/local/bin/perl
print "Content-type: text/html\n\n";
```

Note: **Required:** In the **print** statement, the two newline characters (\n\n) are required to create the required blank line between the CGI headers and your program's output.

Printing the Document Title

The next step is to print the proper HTML codes that will include your document title. These codes will surround your CGI program output. Use Perl **print** statements to print each line. Be sure to print a newline character (\n) at the end of each line of output.

Here is a sample:

```
print "<HTML><HEAD>\n";
print "<TITLE> [Web Clock Output] </TITLE></HEAD>\n";
print "<BODY>\n";
[...]
print "</BODY></HTML>\n";
```

Note: In code segments throughout this book, you will see lines like this:

```
  [...]
```

The ellipses indicate a place where you can fill in your own Perl program statements or HTML code.

Printing the Document Body

Next, we need to print the body of the HTML document. This is usually done in two steps.

1. Assign one or more *document variables.*
2. Use these document variables in double-quoted strings to print the desired body of the HTML document.

Let's go through each of the steps as we write our Web Clock program.

Tip: Whitespace (carriage returns, spaces, and newlines) is not important in HTML.

Assigning Document Variables

For the Web Clock, we will need one document variable to hold the current time. Let's call it *$time.* The Perl function **ctime** will compute the current time and return it as a character string. Since **ctime** is part of the standard Perl library ctime.pl, you can just put in a call to the Perl function **require**:

```
require 'ctime.pl';
$time = &ctime(time);
chop($time);
```

Note: Make sure that your **require** lines are at the top of the program.

The call to **chop**(*$time*) is necessary to remove the newline added by the **ctime** function.

Using Document Variables

Now it's time to create the actual body of the document. First, let's print out the HTML codes to add a major heading for our output:

```
print "<H1>Web Clock Output</H1>";
```

We can now use the *$time* variable to print out the current time:

```
print "<H2>The current time is: $time</H2>\n";
```

The resulting program is given in Listing 4-1:

Listing 4-1: The Web Clock CGI Perl program

```
#!/usr/local/bin/perl
# webclock.pl
require 'ctime.pl';
$time = &ctime(time);
chop($time);
print "Content-type: text/html\n\n";
print "<HTML><HEAD>\n";
print "<TITLE>Web Clock Output</TITLE></HEAD>\n";
print "<BODY>\n";
print "<H1>Web Clock Output</H1>\n"
print "<H2>The current time is: $time</H2>\n";
print "</BODY></HTML>\n";
```

Save this program to a file called webclock.pl. Move it to your script executable directory (/cgi-bin).

Note: Perl source code is plain text, so if you are using a word processor, export your source code to plain ASCII text rather than saving it normally.

Testing the Program

There are two customary ways to test Perl CGI scripts. You can run them in a "stand-alone" mode from a command line, or you can test them directly from a Web page. We recommend you test your scripts in a stand-alone mode for your first efforts in programming CGI with Perl because it's easier to catch errors at this stage. Once the program is bug free, you can test the program from your Web browser.

Running from a Command Line

To run your program from a command line, make sure you, the owner, have permission to execute the program. In UNIX, this is done using the **chmod** command:

```
$ chmod u+x webclock.pl
```

You can now run your program from a command line by typing in the full name of the file:

```
$ webclock.pl
```

This should produce output like the following:

```
Content-type: text/html

<HTML><HEAD>
<TITLE>Web Clock Output</TITLE></HEAD>
<BODY>
<H1>Web Clock Output</H1>
<H2>The current time is: Fri Oct  6 22:29:22 US/Eastern 1995</H2>
</BODY></HTML>
```

When It Doesn't Work

Here we list some of the errors you may encounter when running your program for the first time.

"Not Found"

This error may occur if you are not in the directory where the program resides, or you have not set up your executable search path to include that directory. If you are using UNIX, you'll see the name of your UNIX command shell (we are using Korn shell, **ksh**) followed by a colon (:), the name of the program, and the error. For example

```
ksh:  webclock.pl:  not found
```

To Fix It: Add the directory where your program resides to your executable search path:

```
export PATH="$PATH:/home/CGI/testing"
```

Missing Perl Script Header

If you are using UNIX and forget to include the Perl script header, you will see command shell errors as UNIX tries to execute each line in your Perl program, as if it were a command shell script. You will see errors like the following:

```
webclock.pl[2]: require:  not found
webclock.pl[3]: syntax error at line 4: '(' unexpected
```

To Fix It: At the top of your CGI program, add the header line that gives the location of the **perl** executable. On our system it is

```
#!/usr/local/bin/perl
```

Errors in Syntax

If you create a program with a syntactic error, you will see an error message with the line number where the error was detected, and a description of the error. For example, if you omit the closing single quote on the third line of the Web Clock program, you would see this message:

```
EOF in string at webclock.pl line 3.
```

To Fix It: Make the necessary edits and run your program again.

Using Command-Line Options

If your Perl CGI script is generating CGI output but the output appears to be incorrect, you will want to debug your program before you put it up on the Web. Perl provides a number of option flags to speed up debugging. All of these options are added as flags after the call to **perl** on the command line.

The Execute Option (-e)

When you want to do some quick testing, you can execute Perl commands at the command line using the -e switch, instead of putting them into a script. The following line

```
$ perl -e 'print "Hello World!\n";'
```

will immediately print

```
Hello World!
```

The Warnings Option (-w)

To get warnings about variables that are used before they are set, as well as other potential errors, use the -w switch:

```
$perl -w webclock.pl
```

With the above command, if you forget to assign a value to *$time* before using it, you'll see output like the following:

```
Possible typo: "time" at webclock.pl line 9.
Content-type: text/html

<HTML><HEAD>
<TITLE>Web Clock Output</TITLE></HEAD>
<BODY>
<H1>Web Clock Output</H1>
Use of uninitialized variable at webclock.pl line 9.
<H2>The current time is: </H2>
</BODY></HTML>
```

The Debug Option (-d)

When you want to debug your Perl program, invoke the Perl interpreter with a -d switch:

```
$ perl -d webclock.pl
```

You should see the debugger start up with the first executable line of the program displayed, as shown here:

```
Load DB routines from $RCSfile: perldb.pl,v $$Revision: 4.0.1.3
$$Date: 92/06/08 13:43:57 $
Emacs support available.
Enter h for help.
main'(webclock.pl:3):   require 'ctime.pl';
```

Unlike most debuggers, you can type in and execute any source code while you are in the middle of debugging. Table 4-1 lists some helpful debugging commands.

Table 4-1: Perl Debugger Commands

DEBUGGER COMMAND	MEANING
b *line*	Set a breakpoint at *line* number
d *line*	Delete a breakpoint at *line* number
h	Print help information
p	Print any Perl expression or variable
s	Single-step through your program
t	Turn tracing on and off
T	Print a stack trace

Using the debugger, you can quickly locate what is wrong, type in the necessary Perl commands to fix the problem, and continue with your execution. When your code runs as desired, you can incorporate the code into your source file.

Installing the Program

When you are sure your Perl program works in a stand-alone mode, you are ready to install it on a Web server machine. You need to take the following steps:

1. Identify the correct CGI script directory.
2. Gain write access to this directory.
3. Move your program to this directory.
4. Make your program executable by the Web server.

Identifying a CGI Script Directory

CGI programs reside in a *CGI script directory*, a designated directory on the Web server machine. By convention, CGI programs are usually stored in the /cgi-bin directory. Thus, if your Web server software was installed in the directory /etc/httpd you would find executable CGI programs in /etc/httpd/cgi-bin.

If you do not know where CGI programs are located on the Web server machine you are using, ask your Webmaster or system administrator.

Gaining Write Access

If you are the one who installed your Web server software, you will already have write access to the CGI script directory. Otherwise, you may have to ask your Webmaster or system administrator for access. To make absolutely sure you can access your programs and that they will run without problems, you may want to buy and install a Web server software package of your own.

Caution: **Work with Your Webmaster:** Webmasters usually don't like just anyone running CGI programs on their Web server. A CGI program may slow down other users or applications, crash the Web server, corrupt files, or compromise the security of the computer it is running on. It is best to let your Webmaster test your CGIs before making them generally available from a Web page.

Moving Your CGI Program to the Script Directory

If your CGI program resides on the Web server machine, move your program to the CGI script directory. In UNIX, you would enter a command similar to the following:

```
$ mv webclock.pl /etc/httpd/cgi-bin
```

If you are not working on the Web server machine, you will first have to transfer your program over the Internet to the desired machine, using FTP or another remote file transfer program.

Setting Execute Permissions

The next step is to make sure your program is executable by the HTTP daemon. On UNIX systems, the HTTP daemon often runs as a user called *nobody*. To arrange for this fictitious user to run your CGI programs, you usually have to set execute permissions so that anyone can run your program. For example:

```
$ chmod +x webclock.pl
```

It's best to check with your Webmaster about the proper permissions settings for your CGI scripts.

Running the Program from a Web Browser

Now we are ready to run our program from a Web browser.

No matter where you are on the Internet, simply type the proper CGI URL into your Web browser. For example, if you've installed webclock.pl in the /cgi-bin directory on the Web server machine *www.idgbooks.com*, you can run it as follows:

```
http://www.idgbooks.com/cgi-bin/webclock.pl
```

Tip: **Entering URLs Directly:** Usually there is a place on your Web browser to enter URLs directly. For example, here's what you do in Netscape Navigator 1.1:

1. Select File|Open Location (or use the hotkey Alt+L, or click on the Open icon on the toolbar).
2. Type in the URL to call your CGI program.
3. Press the OK button.

Netscape should run the program and display the results.

All About Aliasing

Aliasing means that the Web server daemon will automatically translate the path part of the CGI URL into an actual sequence of directories and subdirectories on the host machine. With the help of aliasing, users who are publishing Web pages that use CGIs don't have to know the precise location of those CGIs on the remote Web server machines.

CGI program aliasing must be set up by the Webmaster when the Web server is installed.

What You See as Output

If you run your CGI program from the Web browser and all goes well, your Web browser will display a Web page like that shown earlier in Figure 4-2. If the output is not what you expected, it's time to go to work fixing errors.

You may receive the following indications that there are mistakes in your program:

- An error message from the Web server daemon
- Badly formatted output
- Erroneous results

To correct these problems, you'll need to be able to interpret error messages printed by the Web server daemon, identify typical errors in printing HTML codes from Perl programs, and add tracing and debugging messages to your program to locate possible flaws in your program logic.

Interpreting Web Server Daemon Error Messages

When you see a Web page that contains an error message, it is probably your Web server software telling you that your CGI program isn't executing correctly. Each error has a number and a message associated with it. By understanding these messages, you can narrow down what might be wrong.

Table 4-2 lists the seven most common errors that you will encounter when testing your CGI programs and what to do to fix these problems.

Table 4-2: Common Server Errors When Running CGI Programs

ERROR CODE	ERROR MESSAGE	PROBABLE CAUSE	POSSIBLE SOLUTIONS
204	No content	Your CGI script had no output.	Put a **print** statement right after the CGI header to help you see what is going on.
403	Forbidden	Your CGI script is not executable.	Change the execute permissions on your source code.
404	Not found	You misspelled your CGI program's name.	Change the CGI URL or hyperlink, or rename your CGI program file.

(continued)

ERROR CODE	ERROR MESSAGE	PROBABLE CAUSE	POSSIBLE SOLUTIONS
500	Server error	There's a syntax error in your program.	Try running your program from a command line.
502	Bad gateway	You specified incorrect CGI headers.	Fix the first line in your program.
503	Service unavailable	Server is overloaded.	Try a different server.
504	Gateway timeout	Program waiting for input or running in an infinite loop.	Run your program separately.

Identifying and Fixing HTML Format Errors

If you are generating HTML output successfully, but it looks like it's in the wrong format, check to make sure that you are breaking your output lines properly. Printing newlines (\n) in your program will *not* automatically generate line breaks in the browser window. You need to introduce HTML BREAK elements (<BR>) or new paragraphs (<P>), or other HTML codes to start a new line. Check an HTML book or on-line reference for details.

Tracing Your Program

It is often helpful to write tracing messages as HTML comments. For example:

```
print "<!- The time variable=$time -\n";
```

This message will appear in the CGI program's output but will not show up on the Web page display. Use your Web browser's View Source option, if available, to see the HTML comments in the browser window.

Rerunning Your Error-Free CGI Program

After you've fixed errors in your CGI script, you'll want to run it again. You can do this by retyping the CGI URL. Or you can use your Web browser's history feature to resubmit the proper URL to your Web browser.

Tip: An even better way to rerun your program is to reload the current Web page after you have viewed your program's output. In Netscape Navigator 1.1, you can select View|Reload from the menu bar, press the hotkey Alt+R, or click on Reload on the toolbar.

Running Your CGI Program from a Web Page

If you want to provide a better Web user interface to your CGI program, you can create a Web page that calls your program from a hyperlink.

The HTML document in Listing 4-2 includes a hyperlink to the webclock.pl program. Save this file as webclock.html in your Web server document directory.

Listing 4-2: webclock.html, the Web Clock home page

```
<HTML>
<HEAD>
<TITLE>Web Clock Home Page</TITLE>
</HEAD>
<BODY>
<H1>The Web Clock</H2>
As a public service, you can <A HREF="/cgi-bin/webclock.pl">get the
current time</A> from this page.
</BODY>
</HTML>
```

You can now test your CGI program by pointing your Web browser to the URL for this document. When you click on the hyperlink that is displayed, it will run the Web Clock program to generate the same output that you saw in Figure 4-2.

Next, in Chapter 5, we will explore a better way of generating dynamic Web pages. Then in subsequent chapters you'll find out how to use HTML forms and search fields to accept information from users and pass it on to your CGI program.

Chapter 5

Generating Dynamic Web Pages

At this point in the book, you know how to create Web pages in two different ways: from scratch using an editor, and by writing a CGI script that outputs HTML codes.

Here in Chapter 5 we will introduce two more techniques for generating Web pages: server-side includes and page templates.

- With *server-side includes (SSIs),* you insert special commands, in your HTML files. Your Web server software interprets these commands to call CGI scripts.

- With *page templates,* you create your HTML files with special *template variables* as placeholders. Then you write a CGI script to fill in the actual values of these variables.

Using these techniques, you can create fixed HTML files using an editor, and then insert special codes and CGI scripts to add dynamic elements.

Dynamic Pages on the Web

There are many reasons to add dynamic elements to otherwise static Web pages, including the following:

- Page headers, footers, and other dynamic "inserts" can be created once and then included in many Web pages, making those pages more consistent and easier to maintain.

- Late-breaking news and other timely information can be inserted at the last minute.

- By including dynamic data, such as the current file name and last modification date, you can make your Web pages "self-documenting".

Consider the following example of a dynamic page insert. At the Bellcore Web site

```
http://www.bellcore.com
```

a page footer is dynamically included at the bottom of every Web page at the site. Figure 5-1 shows the footer at the bottom of a product information order form.

This footer element includes a toolbar with buttons, hyperlinks to parts of the Web site, a destination for sending feedback to the Webmaster, and copyright information. Copying all this information to each of several hundred HTML files would take a lot of time and be very difficult to maintain. Instead, you can use SSI commands or CGI scripting to dynamically insert the footer at the bottom of each Web page.

Working with Server-Side Includes

Server-side includes (SSIs) are not really part of CGI, but you can use them to fold the output of your CGI scripts into otherwise static Web pages.

Using SSI commands, you can display various dynamic information as part of your HTML files, including

- Values of CGI environment variables
- Information about the current document file
- Size and last modification time of resource files at your Web site

- The entire contents of another HTML file
- The output from a CGI program

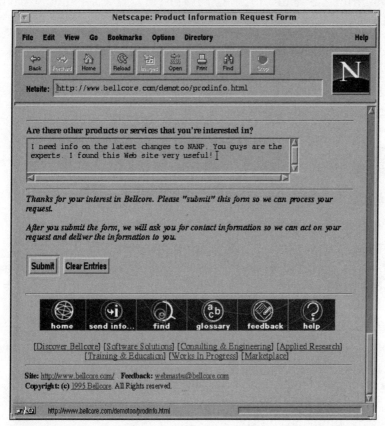

Figure 5-1: Bellcore's Product Information Request Form, with a dynamic page footer at the bottom

The sections that follow describe how to run SSI commands from an HTML source document, and how to turn on SSI processing if it is not currently enabled at your Website. The most popular SSI commands are explained, with examples that you can use on your own Web pages.

A Simple Test: Printing a CGI Environment Variable

First, test if SSI commands work on your system. If your Web server installation permits server-side includes, the server software will automatically scan your HTML files and process the included SSI commands whenever anyone displays that file in their Web browser.

Create a file that includes the following line of HTML:

```
Your client host is: <!-- #echo var="REMOTE_HOST" -->
```

This will print the value of the REMOTE_HOST CGI environment variable:

```
Your client host is: yourmachine.com
```

where *yourmachine.com* is the Internet domain name of the machine you are using.

On the other hand, if you see the following response:

```
Your client host is:
```

then this SSI command is not working properly.

What If It Doesn't Work?

There are several explanations for a broken SSI command:

- Your Web server software does not support the REMOTE_HOST environment variable. This is unlikely, but go ahead and substitute a different CGI environment variable, such as SERVER_NAME or REMOTE_ADDR, and try again.

- Your Web server software doesn't support SSIs, so it is treating the SSI command like a normal HTML comment. This explanation is also unlikely. Most Web server software packages offer some form of SSIs. Check with your Webmaster or your Web server software documentation for instructions on properly formatting the SSI commands on your system.

- Your Web server software supports SSIs, but they are not currently enabled. This is much more likely to be the reason for your unsuccessful test. SSIs are often considered a security risk, so they may be explicitly disabled at your installation.

How to Enable Server-Side Includes

On most Web server software packages, you can turn on server-side includes systemwide by modifying configuration files or selecting a system administration option. To do this, however, you must have special authorization. Check with your Webmaster about local policies regarding use of SSIs.

Configuring the NCSA Web Server for SSIs

On NCSA HTTPd, if you are the Webmaster, you can enable SSIs by adding the following line to /config/access.conf:

```
Options Includes
```

After SSIs are enabled, it is often possible for individual users to turn on SSI processing for selected HTML files in their particular directories. On NCSA HTTPd, users create a special file named .htaccess in the directory where they want to create HTML files with SSI commands. If the .htaccess file contains the following lines:

```
Options Includes
AddType text/x-server-parsed-html .shtml
AddType text/html .html
```

then only files with the .shtml extension will be searched for SSI commands.

Server-Side Include Commands

All SSI commands are HTML comments, with the following general format:

```
<!-- #command tag1="value1" tag2="value2" -->
```

When a user accesses a Web page on a server that has SSIs enabled, the Web server daemon processes each of the SSI commands—even if they are embedded within headings, paragraphs, or other HTML elements. You can use this capability to insert dynamic elements anywhere in your Web page. Let's look at some examples.

Printing Variables with #echo

You can **#echo** CGI environment variables and special SSI variables. Here is an SSI command that prints the date and time in the local time zone, as we did in Chapter 4:

```
<H2>The current time is: <!-- #echo var="DATE_LOCAL" --> </H2>
```

The SSI variable DOCUMENT_URI will display the path to the HTML file for the current Web page:

```
Document: <!-- #echo var="DOCUMENT_URI" -->
```

You can also display the time that the HTML file was last modified, as follows:

```
Last modified on <!-- #echo var="LAST_MODIFIED" -->
```

Using #fsize and #flastmod to Get Information on Resource Files

You can use the **#fsize** command to warn users about the size of media files, as follows:

```
A <A HREF="widget.gif">picture</A> is available
    (size: <!-- #fsize file="image.gif" --> bytes)
```

Use the **#flastmod** command to warn users about a file's age:

```
You can visit our <A HREF="catalog.html"> most recent catalog </A>,
    last updated on <!-- #flastmod file="catalog.html" -->.
```

Inserting Other HTML Files with #include

To include another HTML file with late-breaking news, use the **#include** command:

```
Here is what happened recently at our Web Site: <BR>
    <!-- #include file="news.html" -->
```

Some Web server programs allow you to abbreviate this as follows:

```
<!-- #include "news.html" -->
```

The entire contents of news.html will be inserted into this HTML document at the time the document is accessed by a user.

Using #exec to Display the Output of CGI Scripts

With the **#exec** command, you can even execute a CGI script directly from a Web page. For example, the following line of HTML runs the counter.pl CGI script:

```
You are the <!-- #exec cgi="/cgi-bin/counter.pl" -->th visitor!
```

This script outputs the number of accesses to the current page, producing a message such as

```
You are the 1011th visitor!
```

The cgi tag in this *#exec* command specifies that the output from the CGI script should be inserted directly into this Web page in place of the commented SSI command.

Note: **Web Site:** To get the Perl source code for an access counter CGI script, see
http://www.webtools.org/counter

The cmd tag runs in the following *#exec* command a CGI script without displaying any output, like this:

```
<!-- #exec cmd="/cgi-bin/sendmail.pl" -->
```

Note: **Web Site:** You can get more information about using SSIs with the NCSA HTTPd Web server at
http://hoohoo.ncsa.uiuc.edu/docs/tutorials/includes.html

Things to Consider Before Enabling Server-Side Includes

There is substantial disagreement in the Web community about whether server-side includes should be generally available to Web document authors and CGI programmers. You and your local administrators will have to make your own decisions in this regard. Following are some of the potential drawbacks to using SSIs.

Slower Access to Your Web Pages

Many SSI commands increase the time it takes users to access your Web pages. The Web server software must parse and then process the entire HTML file before displaying anything to the user.

Security Risks

Turning on server-side includes may pose a security risk to your system. Making SSIs available means users who normally can't create and run CGI scripts have the ability to do so. It's easy to mistakenly allow access to CGI scripts that will then compromise a host system's security.

If you are running a high-security Web site, you should disable SSIs entirely. This is fully discussed in Chapter 11, Safe CGI Scripting in Perl.

Resource Limitations

Some Web server software packages limit the size of files that can be included with the SSI *#include* command. This can make SSIs of limited practical use.

No Portability

Unlike conventional HTML files and CGI scripts, Web pages with SSI commands are not usually portable across different Web server installations.

Note: Because of the drawbacks mentioned here, we don't make further use of SSIs in this book. But you can achieve many of the same results using page templates, discussed next.

Working with Page Templates

Page templates are essentially just normal HTML documents containing special markers (template variables) that are later replaced using a CGI script. Each marker begins and ends with two special delimiter characters, such as two exclamation points (!!).

Here is a simple page template that is similar to our first SSI example:

```
Your client host is: !!REMOTE_HOST!!
```

In this example, the template variable is !!REMOTE_HOST!!.

Caution: On the UNIX platform, page template variables are case sensititve. Make sure you use uppercase letters as required.

Your own templates will look a lot like traditional printed "form letters," but with substantial added flexibility provided by your CGI script. Your CGI script must read the page template file, get the value of the template variable, and substitute this value for every occurrence of the variable in the template.

The output from our CGI program using the given page template will be the same as with SSIs:

```
Your client host is: yourmachine.com
```

What You Can Do with Page Templates

Page templates help you create Web pages that contain almost any kind of dynamic information. You're limited only by your programming skills and your imagination. Here are just a few suggestions to get you started:

- Rotate or randomize advertisement graphics to add interest to on-line Webzines and Web news.

- Target your Web pages to particular readers, using information gleaned from CGI environment variables such as the user's e-mail address.

- Calculate prices for products and services, based on the time of day or the number of Web viewers who visit the page.

Creating these kinds of dynamic Web pages would be difficult if you had to program each CGI script from scratch. To make the process much easier, we have created a page template code library for you. It is explained in the next section.

The Page Template Code Library

In this section we present a Perl library called templates-lib.pl. If you you use functions in this library with your CGI script, you will be able to fill templates quickly and easily.

How This Library Works

Listing 5-1 gives the Perl code for our page template library. Save this Perl code to the file templates-lib.pl.

The heart of the template-filling process is in the function **&FillTemplateString.** It takes three parameters:

- *$template:* One long string with the entire contents of the page template file.
- *$delimiter:* A string that holds the special delimiter characters (!!).
- *%varvalues:* An associative array that pairs template variables with their values.

Listing 5-1: Templates-lib.pl, a Perl library for filling templates

```
#!/usr/local/bin/perl
# Templates-lib.pl
# Fills templates that are in files or strings.

# Replaces every "!!var!!" with its corresponding value.
# Actually, the "!!" is a delimiter that can be changed.
# Returns the resulting string.
sub FillTemplateString {
  local($template, $delimiter, %varvalues) = @_;

### Provide default delimiter.
  $delimiter = $delimiter || "!!";
### Add HTML comment for debugging purposes.
  print "<!-- Using template delimiter $delimiter  -->\n";
### Modify $template by substituting in values %varvalues.
### Loop through each template variable.
  foreach $key (keys %varvalues) {
### Substitute the value from the associative array %varvalues into
### the string $template, using global substitution.
    if ($template =~
            s/($delimiter$key$delimiter)/$varvalues{$key}/g) {
      print "<!-- Substituted $key = $varvalues{$key} -->\n";
    }
  }
  return($template);
}


# Reads in the template, separating newlines with spaces.
# Uses FillTemplateString to fill in variables.
# Returns "" if it can't open the template file.
```

```
sub FillTemplateFile {
  local($template_file, %varvalues, $delimiter) = @_;
  local(@template, $template);

### Open a filehandle to the template.
  if (!open(TEMPL, $template_file)) {

### Return immediately if we cannot open the file.
      return "";
  }
  else {

### Read in the whole template, separated by newlines.
    @template = <TEMPL>;
### Join it back together using spaces instead of newlines.
    $template = join(' ', @template);
### Fill in the template.
    $template = &FillTemplateString($template, %varvalues,
$delimiter);
### and return it.
    return($template);
  }
}


1;  # Always return true at end of a library.
```

Installing the Page Template Library

You will be creating several code libraries throughout this book, and
we suggest that you collect them all in one directory that is accessible
to all of your CGI scripts.

Create a directory called /cgi-libs under your CGI script executables
directory. On UNIX, it's

```
$ mkdir /etc/httpd/cgi-bin/cgi-libs
```

Then move the templates-lib.pl there, with

```
$ mv templates-lib.pl /etc/httpd/cgi-bin/cgi-libs
```

The complete path to templates-lib.pl is now

```
/etc/httpd/cgi-bin/cgi-libs/templates-lib.pl
```

Using the Page Template Library

This Perl statement:

```
print &FillTemplateFile("yourtemplate.html", %ENV);
```

will read in your template.html, substitute the values, for template variables that correspond with associative array keys in %ENV, and print out the resulting string.

With the page template library in place, we can use this technique to generate dynamic Web pages that incorporate CGI environment variables, much as we did using the **#echo** SSI command.

A Simple Page Template for Printing a CGI Environment Variable

Let's start by creating the same Web page that we created earlier using server-side includes. We'll need to create the page template file and then the CGI script.

Creating and Installing the Page Template

You can create the page template file using an editor.

```
Your client host is: !!REMOTE_HOST!!
```

Save this file as host.html and install it in a directory where it is accessible by your CGI scripts. On our system, we have created a special directory called templates for just this purpose:

```
$ mkdir /etc/httpd/templates
```

Thus, the complete path to host.html is

```
/etc/httpd/templates/host.html
```

Creating and Installing the CGI Script

Next, create the CGI script to fill in the template. This script must do three things:

- Load the templates-lib.pl code library
- Print a Content-Type CGI header
- Print the string that comes back from &FillTemplateFile

Here is the Perl script that fills in the template:

```
#!/usr/local/bin/perl
# host.pl
require 'cgi-libs/templates-lib.pl';
print "Content-type: text/html\n\n";
print &FillTemplateFile("../templates/footer.html", %ENV);
```

Save this script as host.pl and install it in your executable script directory. You can run it with the following CGI URL:

```
http://www.yourserver.com/cgi-bin/host.pl
```

You should see this output:

```
Your client host is: yourserver.com
```

Use this same technique to add other kinds of dynamic elements to your Web pages.

Things to Consider about Using Page Templates

Page templates have the following advantages over server-side includes.

Efficiency

Page templates are usually more efficient than SSIs. You can substitute for particular markers in particular files. You can also do all substitutions with one CGI script instead of running a script for each desired dynamic element.

Portability

All that's required for the process of using page templates is just to create HTML files and program CGI scripts. Therefore, templates are usually portable across Web server software packages and computing platforms.

Reliability

Because you control the variable substitution using your own CGI scripts, you can make page templates work regardless of the local policies in force at your Web site.

Security

If you follow the guidelines given in Chapter 11, your CGI scripts will be secure. Thus, your dynamic Web pages using page templates will be secure.

The Next Step: Getting User Input

You have now learned two important techniques for creating dynamic Web pages: server-side includes and page templates. However, there are two sides to interactivity: system output and user input. In the next chapter, we will see how to create CGI scripts that accept user input from HTML forms.

Chapter 6

Processing Forms

ill-out forms (we'll just call them *forms*) provide a means for you to add graphical user interface (GUI) components to your Web pages. Form-based Web pages can accept user input and pass it on to CGI programs for processing.

This chapter explains what forms are, how they are used on the Web, how to create them using HTML, and how to write Perl CGI scripts to process their contents. When you are done with this chapter, you should be able to create forms that send e-mail, process on-line orders, and run programs available on your Web server machine. Before we explain forms creation, let's see how forms are being used on the Internet today.

Forms on the Web

On the Web, forms are often used as front-ends to CGI programs that serve as gateways to Internet services, databases, and search engines. Following are some examples of Web sites offering forms used to search technical information, order products, and mail comments to a Webmaster.

A Form for Searching Technical Information

Forms provide a convenient way for users to query databases containing collections of documents. For example, Digital Equipment's Web site provides a fill-out form where users can specify how they want to search various document categories. Figure 6-1 shows this Document Search Engine form. As you can see, users can choose among product descriptions, fact sheets, technical papers, and other information.

The CGI program that runs when you submit this form composes a query to a search engine and formats the results back to the user.

A Form for Ordering Products

One popular use of forms is to provide a way for users to order products and services on the Web. Examples include forms for ordering books, subscribing to magazines, ordering product brochures that can be downloaded and printed, and buying products to be mailed to a home or business.

Product order forms are most effective when they display the products available—like 1-800-USA-GIFT's form for ordering flowers in Figure 6-2. You can view different flower arrangements, select one to order, enter your name, address, and other information, and then click a button to order the product directly from the manufacturer.

The CGI program that runs when you submit a form like this can search customer records, enter information in a database, or send e-mail to the sales department. Most product order forms also display a confirmation page back to the user, indicating whether the order was complete and when to expect a response from the manufacturer.

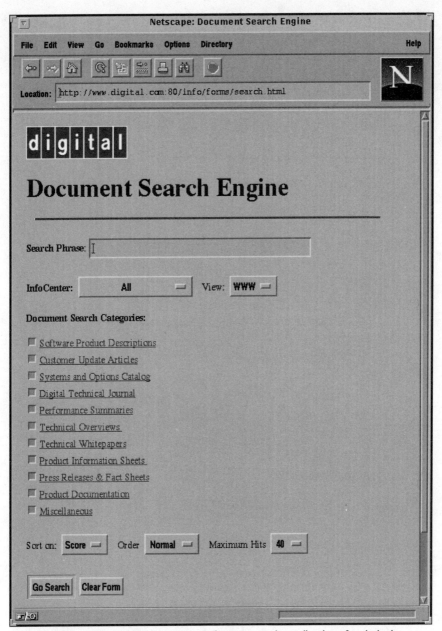

Figure 6-1: Digital Equipment Corporation's form to search a collection of technical documents

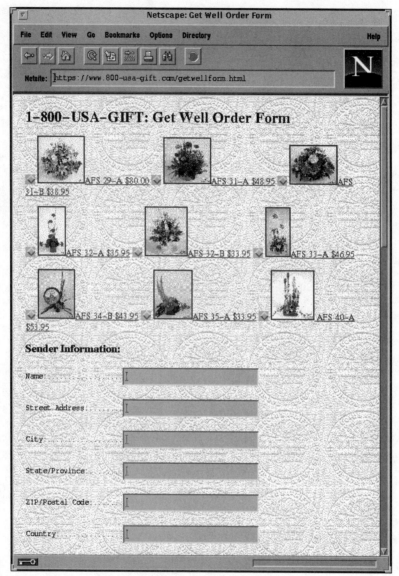

Figure 6-2: The 1-800-USA-GIFT home page offers a form to order flower arrangements

A Form for Entering Comments

Another handy use of forms is for sending comments via e-mail. Figure 6-3 illustrates a comment facility that is part of Bellcore's Web site.

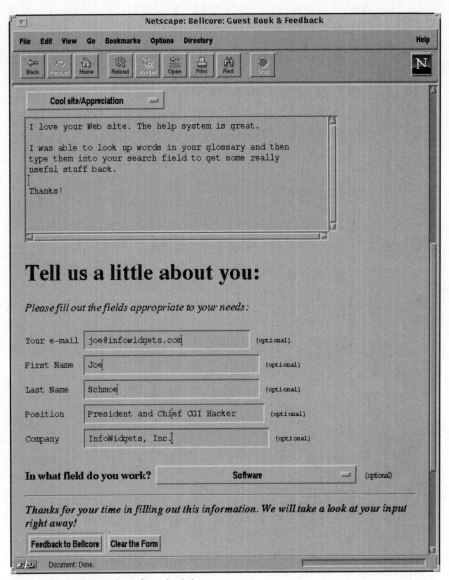

Figure 6-3: Bellcore's form for submitting comments.

The CGI program that runs when you submit this form sends your comments to the site's Webmaster via e-mail.

Four Easy Steps to Creating Forms

The forms feature was introduced in HTML/2.0. Special HTML codes allow you to create text fields, buttons, menus, and other elements that accept input from users. When the user accesses your form-based document with a Web browser, they can fill out the form and submit its contents to a CGI program.

To create any HTML fill-out form, you need to perform the following four steps:

1. Create an HTML document that defines a form.
2. Add graphical input elements for data entry.
3. Add a button for submitting the form to the Web server.
4. Specify the name of a CGI script.

In the sections that follow, we'll create a form that acts as an e-mail gateway. You can offer this form to users of your Web site for sending messages to anyone with an e-mail address on the Internet.

Step 1: Create a Form Document

A form is created using the <FORM> element as shown here

```
<FORM>...</FORM>
```

Forms can appear anywhere within the body of an HTML document.

Step 2: Add User Input Elements

The next step is to add indiviual HTML elements that will accept user input. For our mail form, we will need a single-line text field for entering the e-mail address of our recipient, and a multiline text field for entering the body of the mail message.

Adding a Text Field for an E-mail Address

The <INPUT . . .> element in HTML/2.0 creates all kinds of GUI widgets, including text fields, buttons, and menu entries. A value of "text" for the TYPE attribute tells the Web browser to display a single-line text field. For example

```
<INPUT TYPE="text" NAME="address">
```

A closing tag is not required for the <INPUT> element.

Note: You must *always* include a NAME attribute with each <INPUT> element. The CGI program that processes the form will use the NAME to retrieve the text typed in by the user.

Two other attributes useful for single-line text fields are SIZE and MAXLENGTH.

- SIZE is the width of the field, measured in number of characters.
- MAXLENGTH indicates how far the text field will scroll to permit entry of new characters.

You can also add prompts to tell the user what to input (such as "Please enter an e-mail address") as shown in the following, and field labels (such as "E-mail") to separate fields and permit quick scanning of a complex form.

```
Please enter an e-mail address:<BR>
<STRONG>E-mail:</STRONG>
<INPUT TYPE="text" NAME="address" SIZE=30 MAXLENGTH=50>
```

These form elements are displayed in Figure 6-4.

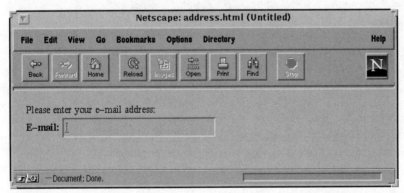

Figure 6-4: A form with an input element that accepts an e-mail address.

Tip: You can omit the TYPE attribute for single-line text fields because "text" is the default field type.

Adding a Text Area for Comments

Now let's add a text area where the user can type in comments, as shown in the form in Figure 6-5. The <TEXTAREA> . . . </TEXTAREA> element allows the user to enter text on more than one line. ROWS and COLS attributes can be added to specify the vertical height and horizontal width of the text area. In this case, the form is 50 characters wide and has 8 lines:

```
<FORM>
Your comments:<BR>
<TEXTAREA NAME="comments" ROWS=8 COLS=50>
</TEXTAREA>
</FORM>
```

Any amount of text can be entered in this field because it will scroll to accommodate more input.

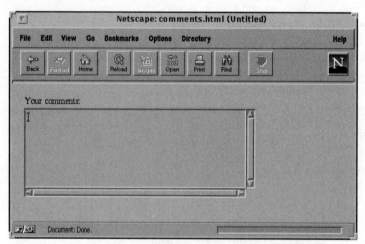

Figure 6-5: A form with a multiline text area for entering comments.

Step 3: Add a Submit Button

The next step is to add a button the user can click to submit input to the Web server. This is done with an <INPUT> element that has a TYPE of "submit". To label the button, you add a VALUE attribute. Here is the HTML tag:

```
<INPUT TYPE="submit" VALUE="Send Comments">
```

Tip: If you have a single <INPUT> element of type "text," a Submit button is not strictly necessary. Pressing Enter anywhere within the form will send the user's input to the Web server.

Step 4: Specify a CGI Script

You can specify a CGI program to process a form by setting the ACTION attribute of the <FORM> element. For example, to have your comments form sent to the comments.pl program on the *www.anyserver.com* Web server machine, you need to add the following ACTION attribute:

```
<FORM ACTION="http://www.anyserver.com/cgi-bin/comments.pl">
```

Listing 6-1 gives the completed HTML for the form.

Listing 6-1: comments.html, the comments form

```
<FORM ACTION="http://www.anyserver.com/cgi-bin/comments.pl">
Please enter an e-mail address:<BR>
<STRONG>E-mail:</STRONG>
<INPUT TYPE="text" NAME="address" SIZE=30 MAXLENGTH=50>
<P>Your comments:<BR>
<TEXTAREA NAME="comments" ROWS=8 COLS=50>
</TEXTAREA>
<P><INPUT TYPE="submit" VALUE="Send Comments">
</FORM>
```

This form—including the e-mail address field, comments box, and Submit button—is displayed in Figure 6-6.

Save this form in an HTML file named comments.html and install it in your Web server's document directory. On our machine, the complete path is

```
/etc/httpd/comments.html
```

Next, we must write the Perl code for comments.pl and install it on our Web server machine. Before we do this, we'll examine how forms are processed, and construct a Perl library that we can use to make processing easy.

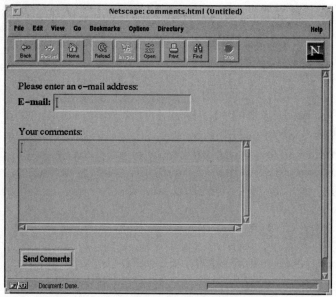

Figure 6-6: The completed form for submitting comments

How Forms Are Processed

What happens when a Web browser user submits a form? In Figure 6-7, you can see how the information entered by the user flows from the client Web browser to the Web server and back. It is a five-step process, as follows:

1. The user fills out the form and presses the Submit button.

2. The client *packs* the form contents into a CGI URL and sends it to the Web server. The CGI URL includes the following items:

   - The domain name of the server

   - A CGI program to run

   - The form contents, packed for delivery

3. The CGI program *unpacks* and processes the form contents.

4. The CGI program sends a response back to the client.

5. The client displays the response to the user.

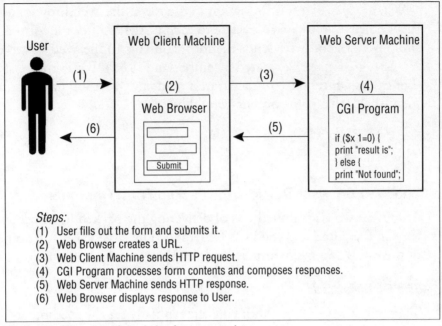

Steps:
(1) User fills out the form and submits it.
(2) Web Browser creates a URL.
(3) Web Client Machine sends HTTP request.
(4) CGI Program processes form contents and composes responses.
(5) Web Server Machine sends HTTP response.
(6) Web Browser displays response to User.

Figure 6-7: Information flow during form processing

Now let's examine the meaning of these terms, *pack* and *unpack*. In this discussion you'll find out how the Web browser packs the contents of the form and delivers it to your CGI program. You'll see how to write Perl programs to unpack the contents of the form, process it, and send back a reply. Also upcoming is a convenient Perl library that you can use to make the unpacking process easier.

The Web Browser Packs the Form Contents

When the user submits a form, the Web browser doesn't send the entire filled-out form to your CGI program. Rather, it just sends the *contents* of the form. To do this, it must identify each element in the form and the information that the user entered into that element. This is done by examining the NAME attributes.

Each NAME attribute must uniquely identify an element of the form. The values of NAME attributes are never displayed to the user; NAMEs are used solely as tags to label the various elements in the form. For example, our e-mail address <INPUT> element had the name "address". The text area for typing comments had the name "comments".

When a user enters information in the form, the Web browser uses this information to assign a value to each NAME. After the form is submitted, the browser sends the form contents to the Web server as "*name=value*" pairs, separated by ampersands (&). For example, if the user enters **whitehouse** in the address field and **great job** in the comments field, the form contents would be

```
"address=whitehouse&comments=great%20job"
```

This is the *packed* form contents.

The Web Browser Delivers the Packed Form Contents

There are two typical methods of delivering the packed form contents: the GET method and the POST method. The METHOD attribute of the <FORM> element tells the Web browser which method to use.

The GET Method

To specify the GET method, you can explicitly set the method attribute to GET:

```
<FORM ACTION="http://www.anyserver.com/cgi-bin/comments.pl"
                METHOD=GET>
```

The GET method will be assumed, however, if you simply omit a METHOD altogether, as in

```
<FORM ACTION="http://www.anyserver.com/cgi-bin/comments.pl">
```

When you submit a form that uses the GET method, you will see an URL such as the following:

```
http://www.anyserver.com/cgi-bin/comments.pl?address=whitehouse&
                                comments=great%20job
```

The form contents appear in the search part of the URL. This URL is a combination of the CGI URL, as specified in the form's ACTION, and the packed form contents, separated by a question mark.

Look carefully at this URL and you'll see that the space between the words *great* and *job* has turned into a special escaped character sequence (%20). (The sidebar, "URL Encoding" tells you why.)

URL Encoding

Because the Web browser includes the entire contents of the form as part of the URL, we say that the contents are *URL encoded*. The browser converts each of the special characters, including spaces and tabs, into the hexadecimal equivalent of their ASCII number, and escapes with a percent sign (%). Thus, a space is converted into the hexadecimal equivalent of ASCII 32 and then escaped, resulting in %20.

Confused? The easiest thing to do is simply look up these special characters in the table, "Encoding Special Characters in URLs" in Chapter 2.

The important thing here is that you are going to need some Perl code to decode the packed form contents before you can use it in your CGI program.

The POST Method

To specify the POST method, you must set the METHOD attribute:

```
<FORM METHOD=POST
    ACTION="http://www.anyserver.com/cgi-bin/comments.pl">
```

Using the POST method, the Web server provides the form contents to the CGI program as if the program were reading from standard input.

Note: **Required:** The value of the METHOD attribute is case sensitive. A value of *post* or *Post* won't work. It must be POST.

Which Method Should You Use?

We highly recommend using the POST method. To find out if the POST method is available on your server, try out a <FORM> element with a METHOD of POST and see if you get

```
Error 405: Method Not Allowed.
```

The CGI Script Unpacks the Form Contents

Before a CGI script processes the form, it generally uses a code library to unpack the form contents.

A number of popular Perl libraries are available on the Web, including Steve Brenner's cgi-lib.pl and Lincoln Stein's CGI.pm. See Chapter 13, Useful Resources, for details. Listing 6-2 gives the Perl code for a basic forms-processing library called forms-lib.pl that provides capabilities similar to these two libraries. We will use forms-lib.pl throughout this book.

The forms-lib.pl code library provides the following function:

- **&GetFormInput()** returns an associative array in which each key of the array corresponds with a NAME attribute in the form, and each value is the corresponding input provided by the user.

This makes it easy to use associative array references to get the values of individual elements of your forms. You can use this function in all of your forms.

Save this listing to a file called forms-lib.pl and move it to your /cgi-libs executable CGI script directory. Our complete path to this library is

```
/etc/httpd/cgi-bin/cgi-libs/forms-lib.pl
```

Listing 6-2: forms-lib.pl, a forms-processing library

```
#!/usr/local/bin/perl
# Forms-lib.pl
# Decodes URLs and unpacks form input.

# Reads the form contents into $input, decodes it,
# unpacks it, and returns it as an associative array.
sub GetFormInput {
  local(%input);
  $input = &ReadInput();
  %input = &ParseInput($input) if $input;
return(%input);
}
# Reads in the form contents and returns it as a string.
sub ReadInput {
  local($method, $input, $length);
  $method = $ENV{'REQUEST_METHOD'};
```

```perl
# 1- If the method is GET, read the searchpart of the URL from
#       the QUERY_STRING CGI environment variable.
  if ($method eq 'GET') {
    $input = $ENV{'QUERY_STRING'};
  }
# 2- If the method is POST, read CONTENT_LENGTH characters
#    from standard input.
  elsif ($method eq 'POST') {
    $length = $ENV{'CONTENT_LENGTH'};
    read(STDIN, $input, $length);
  }
# 3- Return the string.
  return($input);
}
# Takes a URL-encoded string and returns an associative array.
sub ParseInput {
  local($input) = @_;
  local(@pairs);
  # 1- Split into key=value pairs.
  @pairs = split('&', $input);
  foreach $pair (@pairs) {
  # 2- Convert all plus signs to spaces.
    $pair =~ s/\+/ /g;
  # 3- Split into a key and a value.
    ($key, $value) = split('=', $pair, 2);
  # 4- Convert hex numbers to alphanumeric.
    $key =~ s/%(..)/pack("c",hex($1))/ge;
    $value =~ s/%(..)/pack("c",hex($1))/ge;
  # 5- To handle multiple values, separate by newlines.
    $input{$key} .= "\n" if defined($input{$key});
  # 6- Associate keys and values.
    $input{key} .= $value;
  }
  # 7) Return the associative array
return(%input);
}
return 1;  # Always return true at end of a library.
```

6 Easy Steps to Writing Perl Scripts That Process Forms

In this section you'll see how to write CGI scripts to process forms. There are six steps to this process:

1. Add the Perl script header.
2. Require the forms-lib.pl code library.
3. Get the form input as an associative array.
4. Extract necessary data from the associative array.
5. Perform the script's main action.
6. Print a confirmation message to the user.

To illustrate this process, we will write the Perl program named comments.pl. This script will be used to process the Comments form in Listing 6-1. It will get the e-mail address and comments from the form, compose a mail message, send it, and print confirmation that the message has been sent.

Step 1: Add the Perl Script Header

Like all Perl scripts, this one needs a line to tell the command interpreter where to find Perl:

```
#!/usr/local/bin/perl
```

Step 2: Require the forms-lib.pl Code Library

Next, we need to **require** the forms-lib.pl library:

```
require('cgi-libs/forms-lib.pl');
```

Step 3: Get the Form Input

The next step is to get the user's input. We do this by calling the &GetFormInput() function in forms-lib.pl:

```
%input = &GetFormInput();
```

This creates an associative array called *%input,* in which each key corresponds with a NAME in the form.

Step 4: Extract Necessary Data

Next, we need to extract the necessary information from the form input. In this case, we need to get the components of the outgoing mail message from the %*input* array.

The recipient of the mail message will be the e-mail address given in the text field named ADDRESS. We can retrieve the user's entry into this field using an associative array reference, such as

```
$input{'address'}
```

We will send comments to webmaster@*yourserver.com* if no address is specified:

```
$recipient = $input{'address'} || "webmaster@yourserver.com";
```

The body of the mail message will be the comments in the text area element named COMMENTS:

```
$message = $input{'comments'};
```

We also need the e-mail address of the person who is sending the mail, to put in the FROM field of the message. We can get the e-mail address of the Web browser user from the HTTP_FROM CGI environment variable (see Chapter 2). If the browser does not set this variable, we can provide a reasonable substitute:

```
$sender = $ENV{'HTTP_FROM'} || "webmaster@yourserver.com";
```

Step 5: Perform the Script's Main Action

The next step is to perform the script's main action. In this case, we will compose and send a mail message using the UNIX program, **sendmail**. You can substitute any mailer that has a command line interface. Set a string variable to the complete path for the mail program's executable:

```
$MAILER = "/usr/lib/sendmail";
```

A special feature of Perl allows our program to print directly to a program's standard input. We can use this feature to print the contents of our mail message directly to **sendmail**.

```
open(MAIL, "|$MAILER -f$sender $recipient");
```

Note: If you are worried about security at your Web site, consider using the substitutions for **open** suggested in Chapter 11.

Now you can **print** the mail message directly to the MAIL filehandle:

```
print MAIL "To: $recipient\n";
print MAIL "Subject: Comments on your Web Site\n";
print MAIL "\n";
print MAIL $comments;
```

Closing the filehandle will send the e-mail message:

```
close(MAIL);
```

Step 6: Print a Confirmation Message

Finally, we need to print out a simple confirmation message that tells the user that mail has been sent. We'll start with a CGI header, as always:

```
print "Content-type: text/html\n\n";
```

We can use Perl's special string-quoting mechanism to print the confirmation message as an "in-line" HTML document:

```
print <<"EndOfMessage";
<HTML>
<HEAD><TITLE>Comments Sent</TITLE></HEAD>
<BODY>
<H1>Your Comments Were Sent</H1>
The following mail message was sent:
<PRE>
To: $recipient
Subject: Comments on your Web Site

$message
</PRE>
EndOfMessage
```

Installing the Final CGI Script

Listing 6-3 shows the final comments.pl CGI script. Save this program as comments.pl and install it in your Web server's executable script directory. On our machine, the complete path is

```
/etc/httpd/cgi-bin/comments.pl
```

Listing 6-3: The comments.pl CGI script to process a comments form

```perl
#!/usr/local/bin/perl
# comments.pl
# Sends comments via Internet e-mail.

require('cgi-libs/forms-lib.pl');

# Read input from the form.
%input = &GetFormInput();

# Set the recipient, message, and sender.
$recipient = $input{'address'} || "webmaster@yourserver.com";
$message = $input{'comments'};
$sender = $ENV{'HTTP_FROM'} || "webmaster@yourserver.com";

# Specify the mailer
$MAILER = "/usr/lib/sendmail";

# Compose and send the mail message.
open(MAIL, "|$MAILER -f$sender $recipient");
print MAIL "To: $recipient\n";
print MAIL "Subject: Comments on your Web Site\n";
print MAIL "\n";
print MAIL $message;
close(MAIL);

# Print out a confirmation message.
print "Content-type: text/html\n\n";
print <<"EndOfMessage";
<HTML>
```

(continued)

133

```
<HEAD><TITLE>Comments Sent</TITLE></HEAD>
<BODY>
<H1>Your Comments Were Sent</H1>
The following mail message was sent:
<PRE>
To: $recipient
Subject: Comments on your Web Site
$message
</PRE>
EndOfMessage
```

Running the Final CGI Script

After your CGI script is properly installed on your Web server, follow these steps to run it:

1. Bring up the Comments form in an HTML/2.0-capable Web browser using the proper URL, as in

   ```
   http://www.yourserver.com/comments.html
   ```

2. Type in some data. For instance, you'll probably want to enter your own e-mail address and some text, maybe "It really works!" Your Web page should look something like Figure 6-8.

3. Click the Send Comments button. You should see the output in Figure 6-9. If your mailer is functioning correctly, you should also get e-mail.

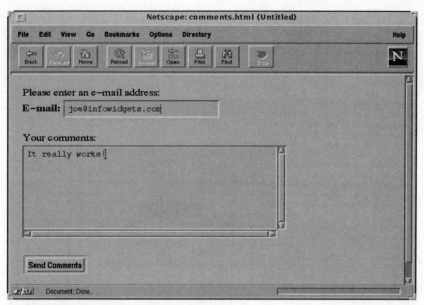

Figure 6-8: Sample input to the Comments form

Figure 6-9: Output from the comments.pl CGI script

Adding Menus to Your Forms

There are three types of menus supported in HTML/2.0: check box menus, radio button menus, and option menus. Check box menus have a "many of many" behavior; the user can check off as many options as needed. Radio button menus have a "one of many" behavior; when a toggle button is selected (pushed down), the last one selected pops up. Option menus can be either single selection or multiple selection.

A form with both radio button and check box menus is shown in Figure 6-10.

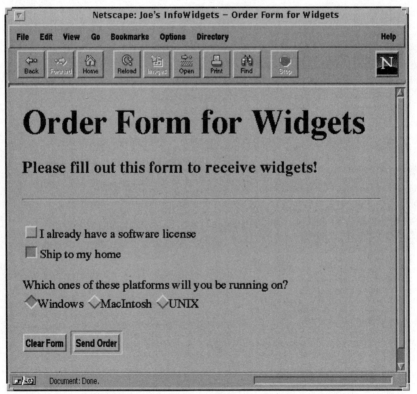

Figure 6-10: A form with check box and radio button menus

Check Box Menus

Check boxes are <INPUT> elements that have a TYPE of "checkbox". Assign a different NAME to each <INPUT> element. For example:

```
<INPUT TYPE="checkbox" NAME="license" VALUE="yes"> I already have a
software license<BR>
<INPUT TYPE="checkbox" NAME="ship" VALUE="yes" CHECKED> Ship to my
home
```

The attribute CHECKED (with no value) specifies that the check box should be checked (toggled on) when the form is initially displayed.

When the form is submitted, if the check box is checked, the VALUE ("yes") is sent as the contents of this <INPUT> element. If it is not checked, no value is sent. For example, if the user deselected the "license" check box and selected the "ship" check box, then the content of the form would be `license=&ship=yes`.

Radio Button Menus

Radio buttons are <INPUT> elements that have a TYPE of "radio". Each radio button should have the same NAME, but different VALUE attributes. For example

```
<P>Which one of these platforms will you be running on?<BR>
<INPUT TYPE="radio" NAME="platform" VALUE="PC" CHECKED>Windows
<INPUT TYPE="radio" NAME="platform" VALUE="Mac">MacIntosh
<INPUT TYPE="radio" NAME="platform" VALUE="UNIX">UNIX
```

Only *one* radio button should be checked using the CHECKED attribute.

The content of the form becomes the NAME paired with the VALUE that was selected. For example, if the Macintosh platform were selected, the form value would be `platform=Mac`.

Single-Selection Option Menus

The <SELECT> . . . </SELECT> element is used to create a menu of options where not all of the options are visible at once:

```
<SELECT NAME="profession">
<OPTION> Applications Programmer
<OPTION> System Administrator
<OPTION> Other
</SELECT>
```

Each OPTION must be given in plain text with no HTML codes.

A form with both single and multiple-selection option menus is shown in Figure 6-11.

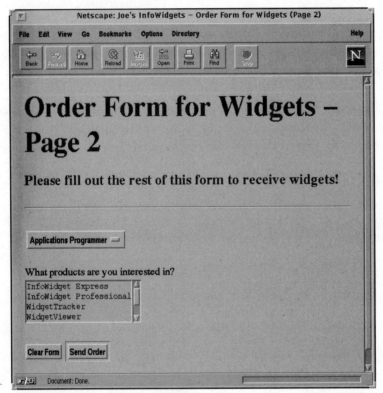

Figure 6-11: A form with two <SELECT> elements

Multiple-Selection Option Menus

The MULTIPLE attribute specifies that users can select more than one option. Here are some form elements that display a multiple-selection scrolling list that always displays two items:

```
<P>What products are you interested in?<BR>
<SELECT NAME="software" SIZE=4 MULTIPLE>
<OPTION> InfoWidget Express
<OPTION> InfoWidget Professional
<OPTION> WidgetTracker
<OPTION> WidgetViewer
<OPTION> WidgetStat
```

```
<OPTION> WidgetAgent
</SELECT>
```

The SIZE attribute specifies how many items are visible. If SIZE is 1, then the options are displayed as a pull-down list. If SIZE is greater than 1, that many items are displayed in a scrolling list. If no SIZE is specified, it defaults to 1.

The contents of the form becomes the NAME paired with each OPTION that was selected. For example, if the software options selected were InfoWidget Express and WidgetAgent, the form value would be

```
software=InfoWidget%20Express&software=WidgetAgent
```

The forms-lib.pl will consolidate these values under one key, named *software,* and separate the values by newlines. Your CGI script can use the **split** operator to get the selected options. For example, if *%input* is an associative array that holds the form contents, then we can get a list of selected options with the following line of Perl code:

```
@options = split("\n", $input{'software'});
```

In Chapter 10, Implementing a Complete CGI Application, you will see an example of a CGI script that uses this technique to process an order form.

Improving Your Forms

This section gives some techniques for improving your forms. You'll see how to provide default values, a Reset button, and password protection.

Providing Defaults

Providing default values gives the user an idea of what can be entered in the field. You can supply a default value for a text field by setting the VALUE attribute:

```
<INPUT TYPE="text" NAME="address" VALUE="name@host">
```

In <TEXTAREA> elements, anything between the <TEXTAREA> and </TEXTAREA> tags is automatically inserted into the text area that is displayed. Here we use a default value to provide instructions:

139

```
<TEXTAREA NAME="comments" ROWS=8 COLS=50>
Enter your comments here.
</TEXTAREA>
```

Providing a Reset Button

Users who frequently work with forms often want to reuse the same form but fill it in with different data. You can add a Reset button as an INPUT element at the bottom of the form, before the Submit button:

```
<P>
<INPUT TYPE="reset" VALUE="Clear Comments">
<INPUT TYPE="submit" VALUE="Send Comments">
```

Clicking on the Reset button clears the form and sets all input elements back to their default values.

Using Password Fields for Sensitive Information

Password fields have a TYPE of "password". They are like text fields except that entered characters are displayed as asterisks (****) on the screen, providing some degree of security. See Chapter 11, Safe CGI Scripting in Perl, for more discussion about the limitations of using passwords for securing your Web resources.

Next Step: Responding to User Input

You have now learned how to create and process forms. Your forms can provide gateways to a wide range of programs available on your Web server machine, including e-mail, newsgroups, databases, and more. In the next chapter, you'll see how to extend the techniques presented here by adding input validation and informative responses to form-processing CGI scripts.

Chapter 7

Providing Informative Responses

Common Gateway Interface (CGI) provides two special headers that you can use to add informative responses to your CGI scripts: the Location header and the Status header. This chapter explains how to write Perl CGI scripts that use these headers to communicate with Web client programs. When you are done with this chapter, you should be able to use these headers to create interactive form-based information services that

- Inform a user when the service is unavailable
- Validate user input
- Generate informative confirmation and error messages

Using CGI Location Headers

The CGI Location header allows you to redirect a Web client program to a resource on your Web server machine or on another Web server across the Internet. For example, in a Perl CGI script the following line

```
print "Location: http://www.anotherserver.com/today/news.html\n\n";
```

will redirect the Web client to the news.html file in the /today directory on *anotherserver*.com's World-Wide Web server.

Note: **Required:** You must include two newlines (\n\n) after printing the last of your CGI headers.

Using a Location header, a Web browser user will automatically see the new Web page—without having to wait for an intermediate Web page to select a hyperlink. This kind of immediate response is important when creating interactive information services.

Printing Location Headers in Your CGI Scripts

The general format for printing CGI Location headers in Perl is

```
print "Location: URL\n";
```

Using Server Redirection

If the desired resource resides on your Web server, your CGI script should print a *relative URL*. For example:

```
print "Location: ../today/news.html\n";
```

The Web server daemon collects the content of the specified file and returns it to the client.

The two periods (..) after "Location:" indicate the parent directory for this file. On our server, CGI scripts will be installed in the /etc/httpd/cgi-bin directory, so this relative path will redirect the Web server daemon to an HTML file in the /etc/httpd directory.

Using Client Redirection

If the desired resource resides on another Web server, your CGI script must print a complete URL. For example:

```
print "Location: http://www.anotherserver.com/today/news.html\n";
```

This is called *client redirection* because the client retrieves the resource on its own.

Using CGI Status Headers

CGI Status headers provide a way for CGI scripts to tell Web browsers and other client programs about the status of the user's request. For example, to inform users that they are unauthorized to access the given resource, your Perl CGI script can **print** an Unauthorized status message:

```
print "Status: 401 Unauthorized\n";
```

Printing Status Headers in Your CGI Scripts

The general format for printing CGI Status headers is

```
print "Status: Code Phrase\n";
```

All *Code* numbers have exactly three digits. The first digit specifies the major category or *level* of status code. For example, level 200 codes indicate that the client's request was successful.

In this section, we examine the three major types of status codes (300, 400, and 500) and explain the use of these codes in Perl CGI scripts. Table 7-1 is a summary of the status codes and phrases most often used in CGI scripts. See also Table 4-2 in Chapter 4 for the most common status codes seen when running CGI scripts.

Table 7-1: Status Codes and Phrases Used in CGI Scripts

CODE	PHRASE	MEANING
300	Multiple choices	Your script is providing a list of available locations for the requested resource.
301	Moved permanently	Your script is using the Location header to tell the client the requested resource's new location.
302	Moved temporarily	Your script is using the Location header to tell the client a temporary place to find the requested resource.
400	Bad request	Your script is telling the client that their request had a bad syntax, was missing information, or had some other problem.
401	Unauthorized	Your script is telling the client they need a password to access this resource.
500	Internal server error	You have reached an error state in your CGI script.

Level 300 Status Codes (Redirection)

When you print a Location header, you can also print a level 300 status code to inform the client that the resource has Moved Permanently (301) or Moved Temporarily (302). For example, to indicate that samefile.html has permanently moved to *anotherserver*.com's Web server, you would use the following lines:

```
print "Status: 301 Moved Permanently\n";
print "Location: http://www.anotherserver.com/samefile.html\n\n";
```

If there are several possible new locations for the resource, you can print the Multiple Choices (300) status code and provide a list of URLs.

Level 400 Status Codes (Client Errors)

Level 400 status codes mean that the client's request is insufficient in some way. For example, your script may detect that the user has not supplied a required form entry. In this case, it can print a Bad Request (400) status message:

```
print "Status: 400 Bad Request\n";
```

Or your script may determine that a client does not have proper authorization to run your service. In this case, you can generate an Unauthorized (401) status message:

```
print "Status: 401 Unauthorized\n";
```

Level 500 Status Codes (Server Errors)

The level 500 status codes mean that your CGI script can't properly process the client request. For example, the script may detect an error opening a required file. The script should print an Internal Server Error (500) and return immediately with an empty string (""). For example:

```
print "Status: 500 Internal Server Error\n\n";
return("");
```

Note: If an error occurs in running your CGI script, such as a Perl syntax error, the Web server daemon automatically returns a Bad Gateway (502) message informing the client about the problem.

Displaying an "Out of Service" Message

Now let's put to work what you've learned about Location and Status headers, by writing some CGI scripts in Perl.

Suppose you are creating a home page on the Web, but it isn't ready yet. You want would-be users to see something friendlier than a nasty Web server error message or a badly formatted display. You can provide an "Out of Service" message, instead, to let them know what is going on while you're finishing your work. See Figure 7-1.

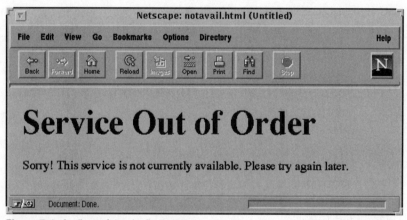

Figure 7-1: An "out of service" message

We will use the Location header to redirect the client browser to an HTML file named notavail.html on our Web server. The file will contain the "Out of Service" message, along with the Status header to warn the client that this redirection is only temporary.

Creating the CGI Script

Create your CGI script as you did in the last chapter. Start with the usual Perl commented header line:

```
#!/usr/local/bin/perl
```

Print the status code and phrase to indicate temporary redirection:

```
print "Status: 302 Moved Temporarily\n";
```

Print the CGI Location header and provide it with the relative path to the desired file:

```
print "Location: ../notavail.html\n\n";
```

Save this CGI script as service.pl and install it in your executable CGI script directory. On our system, the full path to this script is

```
/etc/httpd/cgi-bin/service.pl
```

Listing 7-1 gives the Perl source code.

Listing 7-1: service.pl, an example using the CGI Location header to redirect to other HTML files

```perl
#!/usr/local/bin/perl
# service.pl
# REMOTE_HOST - The machine name of the connecting client machine.
#               Example: infowidget.com
# SERVER_NAME - The full domain name of the server machine.
#               Example: infowidget
$server = $ENV{'SERVER_NAME'};
$host = $ENV{'REMOTE_HOST'};
# Does server's address begin with the remote host's name?
if($server =~ /^$host/i) {
    print "Location: ../service.html\n\n";
}
# otherwise, redirect to the "Out of Service" message.
else {
  print "Status: 302 Moved Temporarily\n";
  print "Location: ../notavail.html\n\n";
}
```

Testing the CGI Script

Once our service is up and running, we'll want to display our home page. Create a sample home page, such as the following:

```html
<HTML>
<HEAD><TITLE>Joe's InfoWidgets</TITLE></HEAD>
<BODY>
```

```
Welcome to Joe's InfoWidgets!
</BODY>
</HTML>
```

Name this file service.html and install it in your Web server document root directory. On our system, the full path to this file is

```
/etc/httpd/service.html
```

Next, create an HTML file containing the "Out of Service" message. The body of this file should look something like this:

```
<H1> Service Out Of Order </H1>
Sorry! This service is not currently available. Please try again later.
```

Name this file notavail.html and install it under your document root directory. On our machine, the complete path is

```
/etc/httpd/notavail.html
```

Now run your CGI script from a Web browser. On our system, we would type in the following CGI URL:

```
http://www.yourserver.com/cgi-bin/service.pl
```

If your Web browser is running on the Web server machine, you should see Joe's InfoWidgets home page. If your Web browser is running on a client machine other than the server, you should see the notavail.html document as it appears in Figure 7-1.

Displaying Confirmation and Error Messages

Now let's add a confirmation message to the comments.pl CGI script from Chapter 6 (Listing 6-3).

Creating a Confirmation Message

First, create an HTML document that will confirm a successful response, like that shown in Listing 7-2.

Listing 7-2: A confirmation document

```
<HTML>
<HEAD><TITLE>Your Comments Sent</TITLE></HEAD>
<BODY>
<H1>Your Comments Were Sent</H1>
Thank your for your comments.
<P>Your mail has been sent.
</BODY>
</HTML>
```

Save this confirmation document as comments_confirm.html and install it in a location that can be accessed by your Web server. On our server, we have created a special directory for these files under our document root directory called /responses. The complete path is

```
/etc/httpd/responses/comments_confirm.html
```

Redirecting to a Confirmation Message

After the main portion of your CGI script (the Script Action), you can print a Location header to redirect the Web server to the confirmation document. For example:

```
# Compose and send the mail message.
# Respond by displaying comments_confirm.html.
print "Location: ../responses/comments_confirm.html\n\n";
}
```

Adding Error Messages

In Chapter 3, Perl: A Good Language for CGI Programming, we showed you how to display error messages using the Perl **die** operator. Unfortunately, using this method does not automatically pass the error message on to the client. You can, however, create your own catalog of error documents and use redirection to display them when an error condition occurs.

For example, suppose the user doesn't fill out an e-mail address in the Comments form in Listing 6-1. You might want to display the error document, shown in Listing 7-3.

Listing 7-3: comments_err_no_addr.html, an error document

```
<HTML>
<HEAD><TITLE>Comments Not Sent: Missing Address</TITLE></HEAD>
<BODY>
<H1>Comments Not Sent</H1>
This program will not deliver mail without the address filled in.
<P>Please return to the form and fix this problem.
<P>No comments were sent.
</BODY>
</HTML>
```

Save this document as comments_err_no_addr.html. On our server, the complete path is

```
/etc/httpd/responses/comments_err_no_addr.html
```

Adding Tests for Error Conditions

In the Perl script that processes the form, you may want to add tests to check for error conditions. Be sure to position them *before* the main part of the program (the script action).

For example, to add a test for an empty ADDRESS field, we need to get rid of the default value for *$recipient:*

```
# Get the recipient from the ADDRESS field.
  $recipient = $input{'address'};
```

and then test if *$recipient* is set to the empty string

```
# Test for an empty string.
  if ($recipient eq '') {
```

Redirecting to the Appropriate Error Message

Now that we've determined if the e-mail address was left blank, let's redirect to the appropriate error message.

As the action part of the test, add a Location header to redirect the Web server to the appropriate error document. For example

```
# Redirect to the error document
  print "Location: ../responses/comments_err_no_addr.html\n\n";
  }
```

149

After all the tests for error conditions have been done, add an **else** clause that performs the script action and redirects to the confirmation document. Notice that we have moved the script action to a separate function named &SendMessage:

```
else {
  &SendMessage($sender, $recipient, $message);
  print "Location: ../responses/comments_confirm.html\n\n";
  }
```

Putting It All Together

The full code for comments.pl with a confirmation message and error checking is given in Listing 7-4.

Save this script as the new version of comments.pl and install it in your executable script directory. Our complete path is

```
/etc/httpd/cgi-bin/comments.pl
```

Listing 7-4: The Comments Form CGI script with confirmation and error message responses

```perl
#!/usr/local/bin/perl
# comments.pl
# Sends comments via Internet e-mail.
# -- Added confirmation and error messages
require('cgi-libs/forms-lib.pl');
$SERVER_NAME = $ENV{'SERVER_NAME'};
MAIN: {
    # Read input from the form.
    %input = &GetFormInput();
    # Set the recipient, message, and sender.
    $recipient = $input{'address'};
    $message = $input{'comments'};
    $sender = $ENV{'HTTP_FROM'} || "webmaster@yourserver.com";
if ($recipient eq '') {
    print "Location:    ../responses/comments_err_no_addr.html\n\n";
}
else {
    &SendMessage($sender, $recipient, $message);
    print "Location: ../responses/comments_confirm.html\n\n";
```

150

```
    }
}
# Send the mail message.
sub SendMessage {
    local($from, $to, $msg) = @_;
    local($mailer);
    $mailer= "/usr/lib/sendmail";    # Specify the mailer
    open(MAIL, "|$mailer -f$from $to");
    print MAIL "To: $to\n";
    print MAIL "Subject: Comments on your Web Site\n";
    print MAIL "\n";
    print MAIL $msg;
    close(MAIL);
}
```

Testing the CGI Script

Refer to the directions in Chapter 6, Processing Forms, for running this CGI script from the Comments form. If a user submits the Comments form without filling in an e-mail address, an appropriate error message will be displayed. Once everything is filled in, the confirmation message will appear.

We will use this script again in Chapter 10, Implementing a Complete CGI Application, to provide a comments facility for our shopping service's storefront page.

What's Next?

At this point you have studied how to create interactive forms that accept and validate user input and provide informative confirmation and error messages. Now let's take a look at the other major category of CGI scripts covered in this book: search gateways.

## Chapter 8

Adding Search Capabilities

T he wealth of the World-Wide Web's information resources, unfortunately, provides little organization for the user wanting to find something specific. When you know exactly what you need, surfing through a maze of hyperlinks is slow and costly. *Search gateways* are an efficient way for users to locate relevant resources more quickly, by letting them specify what they want to find.

This chapter defines search gateways and explains how they work, describes how they are used on the Web today, and shows you how to write your own search gateway scripts using Perl.

What Is a Search Gateway?

A search gateway is a CGI program that accepts a request for information from a user, the *search request,* and returns a list of relevant resources, the *search results.* These resources can be documents, programs, structured files, or almost any kind of information. They may reside on a given Web server or be located at various Web servers across the Internet.

Think of the search gateway as performing the role of a busy information desk. You ask a question, such as, "Where do I buy an Internet search engine?" In response, you receive pointers to relevant locations where you may be able to find the information you've requested.

The Search Request

Most search gateways require the user to enter the search request as a set of *keywords,* such as

```
Internet, search, engines
```

that is likely to match words in the desired resources. Some search gateways translate these keywords into a *query*

```
(Internet OR Search OR Engines)
```

in a specialized query language such as Standard Query Language (SQL). The user may also be able to enter terms from the query language directly, to add more precision to their search criteria, as in

```
(Internet AND (search AND (engines OR gateways)))
```

The best search gateways accept search requests in plain English and automatically translate them into the query language, freeing the user from having to learn a query language at all.

The Search Engine

Search gateways usually pass the query to a separate program, the *search engine,* that does the real work of matching the query against the text in the various resources. There are many public-domain and commercial search engines available, including those from Fulcrum, Verity, Personal Library Software, and Open Text.

Web Site: Yahoo! provides a fairly comprehensive list of companies selling search engines at `http://www.yahoo.com/Computers_and_Internet/WWW/SearchEngines`

The Search Results

Search engines usually return a list of resources in order of relevance. Relevance is usually defined by the overlap between the keywords in the query and the text contained in the resource. For the example search query mentioned just above (Internet, search, engines), a company's product page might be listed first, because it mentions the words *Internet, search,* and *engines* all in the same document.

The search gateway must translate the search engine's list of re-sources into something that the user can view. Usually search gateways return the search results as an HTML document that consists of hyperlinks to URLs (such as company home pages). The user need only read the titles or short descriptions of each resource and then select the desired hyperlinks to view the full text of the documents.

Later, we'll see a graphic representation of the relationship between these search gateway elements.

Search Gateways on the Web

Let's take look at what search gateways are available on the World-Wide Web today. Along the way, we'll introduce some powerful search engines that you can use at your Web site.

Search gateways on the Web typically support one of the following activities:

• Searching a Web site for HTML documents

• Searching a database of similar, structured resources

• Searching the entire Web for a variety of resources

This section explains each type of program and gives examples and pointers to relevant software.

A Search Facility for a Web Site

Probably the most popular use of a search gateway is to provide fast access to the documents stored on a Web server. Figure 8-1 shows the search form from Bellcore's Web site. This search facility was built using the Harvest search engine (see sidebar "About Harvests"). It helps users quickly locate any of the Web pages at the Bellcore site.

Search the Bellcore Website

This search engine was built using Harvest

Search for the terms: Internet Search Engines

Perform Search   Clear Form

Figure 8-1: Bellcore Web site search facility, built using the Harvest search engine

Figure 8-2 shows the output from our search request "Internet search engines."

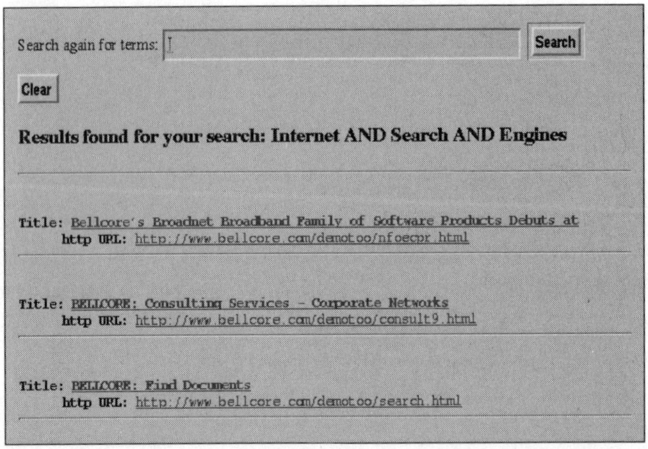

Search again for terms: [ ] Search

Clear

Results found for your search: Internet AND Search AND Engines

Title: Bellcore's Broadnet Broadband Family of Software Products Debuts at
       http URL: http://www.bellcore.com/demotoo/nfoecpr.html

Title: BELLCORE: Consulting Services - Corporate Networks
       http URL: http://www.bellcore.com/demotoo/consult9.html

Title: BELLCORE: Find Documents
       http URL: http://www.bellcore.com/demotoo/search.html

Figure 8-2: Output from a Harvest search of the Bellcore Web site

The Harvest system has located several documents that mention *some* of the keywords entered by the user in the search form. These documents are listed in order of relevance. Notice the hyperlinks that let users jump directly to the documents they need.

About Harvest

Harvest is public-domain software from the University of Colorado:

```
http://harvest.cs.colorado.edu
```

Harvest provides an efficient architecture for gathering and replicating collections of resources across multiple Web servers.

A Search Gateway to a Database

Another popular use for a search gateway is accessing database servers that maintain collections of related Web resources. Such databases store structured information—telephone and fax numbers for employees, movie reviews and ratings, or bibliographies that list author, publisher, and date of publication.

WAIS

The most popular database server on the Web is WAIS (Wide Area Information Service). The following versions of WAIS are available:

- *freeWAIS*—a basic, public-domain version of WAIS

```
ftp://ftp.germany.eu.net/pub/infosystems/wais/CNIDR
```

- *freeWAIS-sf*—an enhanced freeWAIS distribution that supports structured searches

```
http://ls6-www.informatik.uni-dortmund.de/freeWAIS-sf
```

- *Commercial WAIS*—the commercial product available from WAIS, Inc., that provides more sophisticated searching techniques and better performance

```
http://www.wais.com
```

Search Gateways That Access WAIS

Several public-domain search gateway programs are available that will access WAIS databases, including:

- *DocFinder*—a gateway to freeWAIS databases; from NCSA; written in Perl

```
http://docfinder.ncsa.uiuc.edu:7999
```

- *Sfgate*—a more full-featured Perl program for accessing free WAIS-sf databases

```
http://bib.informatik.uni-dortmund.de/SFgate
```

Figure 8-3 shows an input form for Sfgate, configured to search an archive of bibliographic references. This Sfgate demo is at

```
http://ls6-www.informatik.uni-dortmund.de/SFgate/demo.html
```

Figure 8-4 shows the output when we entered the query "Internet search engines," an author of "Krol," and a publication date after 1990. Notice that recent publications about the Internet by Ed Krol top the list.

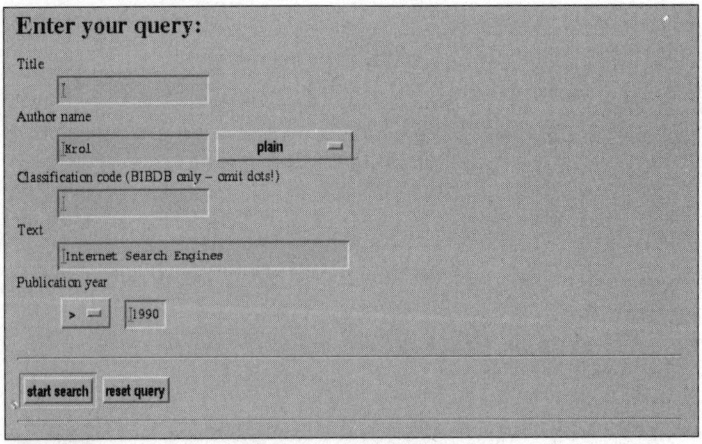

Figure 8-3: The Sfgate database search gateway

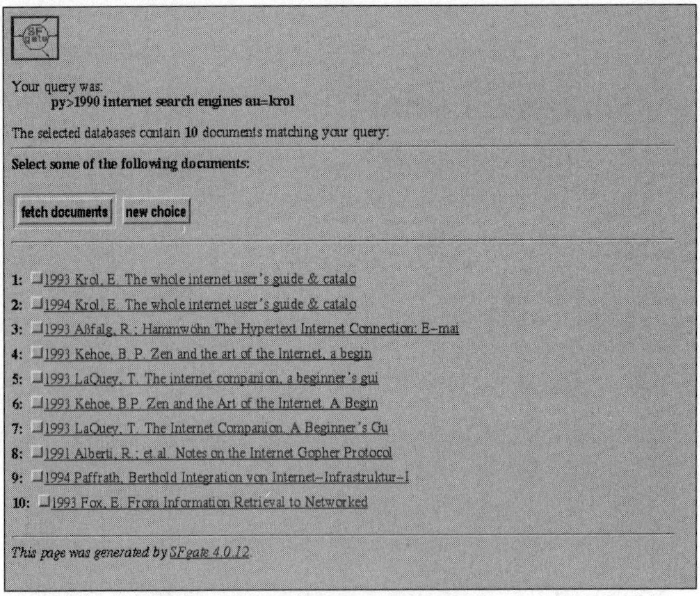

Figure 8-4: Output from our SFgate query in Figure 8-3

There are also several public-domain and commercial search gateways provided by database companies, including Oracle and Sybase. See Chapter 12, Where to Go from Here, for more information on these products.

A Searching Service for the Web

Perhaps the most popular use of search gateways is to provide an information service for searching the entire World-Wide Web. There are dozens of Web-searching services now available, including Digital's AltaVista, InfoSeek, Galaxy, and Excite!

The commercial Web-searching services use a *gatherer* or *web spider* program that "walks" the Web, visiting different sites and gathering relevant resources.

LYCOS

One of the most comprehensive Web-searching services is LYCOS, at

```
http://www.lycos.com
```

Figure 8-5 is a LYCOS input form. Figure 8-6 shows the output from LYCOS when we input the query "Internet Search Engines." In this example, we have set the search controls to create a summary instead of listing all lines that match the query. Notice that Web pages specifically about Internet search engines top the list.

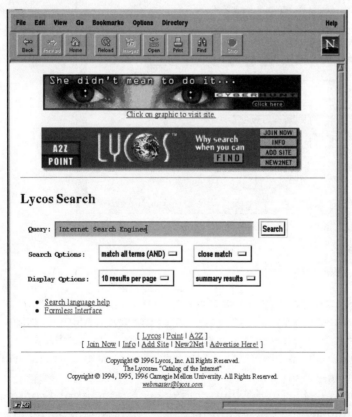

Figure 8-5: Doing a search with LYCOS, a World-Wide Web searching service

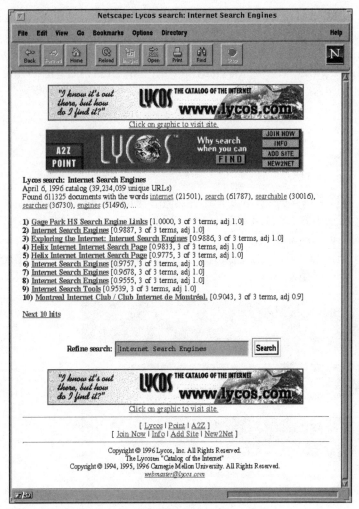

Figure 8-6: Output from the LYCOS search in Figure 8-5

How Search Gateways Work

Whether a search gateway is searching a Web site, a database, or the entire Web, the gateway must be able to understand queries, collect resources, match queries to resources, and display the results. This section explains the components of a search gateway and the information flow among them.

The diagram in Figure 8-7 illustrates the components of a complete Web-searching facility. The following events (indicated in the numbers in parentheses in figure 8-7) take place when a user runs a search gateway:

160

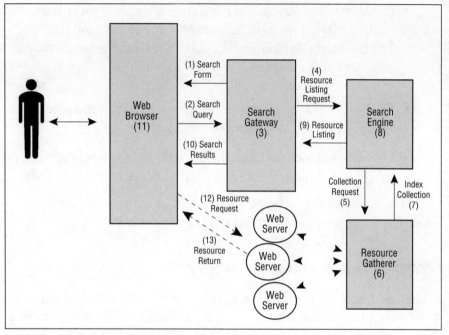

Figure 8-7: Components of a Web search facility

- The search gateway sends a search form (1) to the user's Web browser.

- The user inputs a search query, keywords, or English text (2).

- A search gateway accepts the search query (3) and composes a resource listing request (4).

- (5) The search engine accepts the resource listing request and performs the search. This may involve accessing a database of resources that has been already created, or calling the resource gatherer to generate a new resource database.

- The resource gatherer collects resources from one or more Web servers (6) and extracts a searchable subset of the resource, to create an index collection (7).

- The search engine matches the query against the contents of each index in the index collection (8) and returns a resource listing (9). The resource listing provides URLs for the resources that matched the query and lists them in rank order of relevance.

- The search gateway uses the resource listing to generate search results (10) that include details about the match and where to find the original resources (URLs). The search gateway may also group or summarize the resources, highlight matched keywords, or indicate degree of match.

- The user views the search results through a Web browser and selects hyperlinks that seem promising (11).

- The Web browser requests the URLs from the original Web server (12), and the server returns the full resource to the user (13).

The user can then browse the full text of the resource, select a different resource, or input another search request.

Creating a Search Gateway Using Perl

In this section, you will see a simple search facility created using Perl's file-manipulation and string-matching facilities. The search facility will include the following components. You can use these components together to provide a search facility for your Web site.

- *Search form.* An HTML document that uses the <ISINDEX> tag to activate the Web browser's built-in search feature.

- *Resource gatherer.* A Perl library, gatherer-lib.pl, that gathers resources. Uses two other Perl libraries that we introduce later: database-lib.pl, to access HTML documents using the local file system, and indexer-lib.pl, to extract the searchable index text in those files.

- *Search engine.* A Perl library, searcher-lib.pl, that scores each document and then rank-orders them all. Matches each keyword in the query against the extracted index text, using exact string matching.

- *Search gateway.* A CGI script that accepts queries input to the search form and displays the titles of those documents with index text that best matched the query. Includes hyperlinks to the full documents. Uses the indexer-lib.pl Perl library to extract the searchable text from the HTML document.

The Search Form

The search form is an HTML document that accepts the user's query. You can provide a simple search form using the <ISINDEX> tag. When a browser displays a document with an <ISINDEX> tag, the tag activates the browser's built-in search feature. This kind of search form is usually sufficient for simple keyword queries.

Figure 8-8 shows how a Web browser displays an ISINDEX document. You can see that the Web browser has automatically supplied a search prompt and search request entry field. If you press Enter anywhere within the browser window, the browser will pass the search keywords entered in the search field to your search gateway script.

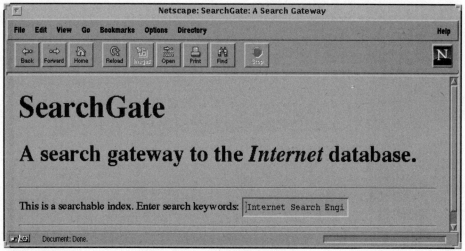

Figure 8-8: The search form created with an ISINDEX document

The Resource Gatherer

The *resource gatherer* is a software component that gathers together resources from one or more Web servers and centralizes them for the search engine.

Listing 8-1 shows the code for our resource gatherer, a Perl library called gatherer-lib.pl. This library will accommodate various ways of retrieving and indexing resources. It provides the following function:

- **&GatherResources(*$database*)** returns a list of resources associated with the given database.

Listing 8-1: The Perl library, gatherer-lib.pl, a resource gatherer

```perl
#!/usr/local/bin/perl
# gatherer-lib.pl
# A generic resource gatherer.

require 'database-lib.pl';  # plug in database retriever
require 'indexer-lib.pl';   # plug in indexer

# Returns a list of resource names in the database while caching the
# headlines and indices for later access.
sub GatherResources {
  local($database) = @_;
  local($contents, $index, @resources);

  # Get the list of resources in the database.
  @resources = &GetDatabaseResources($database);

  # Extract and cache the index and headline for each resource.
  foreach $resource (@resources) {
        print "<!-- Searching $resource -->\n";
        $contents = &GetDatabaseResource($database, $resource);
        &StoreResourceIndex($resource, $contents);
        $index = &GetResourceIndex($resource);
        &StoreResourceHeadline($resource, $index, $contents);
  }
  return(@resources);
}
1; # always return 1 from libraries
```

The Search Engine

The *search engine* is a software component that matches the user's query against each index in the collection created by the resource gatherer.

Listing 8-2 provides a Perl library called searcher-lib.pl. This library implements a simple search engine that offers keyword matching. This library provides the following functions:

- **&SearchResources($*query*, @*resources*)** matches the the *query* against the indices of the given *resources* and returns the list of resources, rank-ordered by score.

- **&GetResourceScore($*resource*)** returns the numeric score associated with the given *resource.*

The searcher-lib.pl library's internal functions are the only ones specific to keyword searching. They sum the number of occurrences of each keyword in the index text associated with the resource.

Listing 8-2: The Perl library searcher-lib.pl, a search engine

```perl
#!/usr/local/bin/perl
# Searcher-lib.pl
# A generic search engine.

require 'database-lib.pl';  # plug in database retriever
require 'indexer-lib.pl';  # plug in indexer

%SCORES = ();

# Numeric scores indexed by resource.
# Returns a rank ordered summary list of resources.
sub SearchResources {
    local($query, @resources) = @_;
    local($resource, $index, @ordered);
    local(@query) = split(' ',$query);
    print "<!-- Matching resources: @resources against $query -->\n";
    # For each resource, retrieve the index and compute a score.
    foreach $resource (@resources) {
        $index = &GetResourceIndex($resource);
```

(continued)

```perl
        &StoreResourceScore($resource,
                            &MatchQuery($index, @query));
    }
    # Order resources by their score.
    @ordered = sort byscore @resources;
    print "<!-- Ordered resources: @ordered -->\n";
    return(@ordered);
}
# Gets the score associated with a given resource from %SCORES.
sub GetResourceScore {
  local($resource) = @_;
  return($SCORES{$resource});
}
# Stores the score for the given resource in %SCORES.
sub StoreResourceScore {
    local($resource, $score) = @_;
    $SCORES{$resource} = $score;
}
# ---- Internal functions for the search engine ----
# Returns a matching score for a given document based on the number
# of occurrences of each keyword in the $index.
sub MatchQuery {
    local($index, @query) = @_;
    local($text);
    local($matches) = 0;
    foreach $word (@query) {
        $temp = $index;            # Reset the temporary string.
        while ($temp=~/$word/i) {  # Case-insensitive match.
            $matches++;            # Count matches.
            $temp = @';            # Advance past the match.
        }
    }
    print "<!-- Got $matches matches between @query AND $index -->\n";
    # Return the total number of matches of all keywords.
    return($matches);
}
```

```
# Compares numeric scores for resources. $a and $b are reserved
# variables used by Perl for matching. Not clean, but efficient.
# <=> does a signed comparison and -1 flips it so we get the largest
# values first in our sort.
sub byscore {
    return((&GetResourceScore($a) <=> &GetResourceScore($b)) * -1);
}
1; # Always return 1 from libraries.
```

The Search Gateway Script

The search gateway connects the search form with the search engine. In this section, we explain how to access the user's query, print the search form, and access the name of a database to search. We will then give the code for SearchGate, our sample search gateway script written in Perl.

Accessing the Query

With search forms created using ISINDEX documents, the query is a set of search word. Each search word is passed as a separate command-line argument. Thus, when the user types "Internet Search Engines" into the search field, it's equivalent to executing the following code at a command-line prompt:

```
$ searchgate.pl Internet Search Engines
```

Note: The search terms are *not* URL encoded, so you don't have to worry about special characters such as plus signs (+). Each of the search words is a string of alphanumeric characters with no spaces or newlines.

Your CGI script can use the predefined array @ARGV to access each of the words.

Printing the Search Form

To create a working search facility, you must create a CGI script that first checks to see if there are any command-line arguments, and then prints the search form if there are none. For example

```
if (! $ARGV[0]) {
  ...Print HTML codes here ...
}
```

Listing 8-3 is searchgate.pl, a CGI script that provides a generic search interface to a database of unstructured text resources.

Listing 8-3: The searchgate.pl script, a general search gateway script

```
#!/usr/local/bin/perl
# searchgate.pl
# SearchGate, a generic search facility.

require ('database-lib.pl'); # plug in a database retriever
require('gatherer-lib.pl'); # plug in a gatherer
require('searcher-lib.pl'); # plug in a search engine

MAIN: {
    # Get the database from PATH_INFO.
    $database = substr($ENV{'PATH_INFO'}, 1);
        if (! $database) {
  print "Location:
 ../responses/searchgate_err_no_database.html\n\n";
        exit(1);
    }
    print "Content-type: text/html\n\n";
    print "<!-- Searching database: $database -->\n";
    if (! $ARGV[0]) {    # If no arguments, print search form in-line.
  print <<"EndOfSearchForm";
        <HTML>
        <HEAD><TITLE>SearchGate: A Search Gateway</TITLE>
        </HEAD>
        <BODY>
        <H1>SearchGate</H1>
        <H2>A search gateway to the <EM>$database</EM> database.</H2>
        <ISINDEX>
        </BODY></HTML>
EndOfSearchForm
}
    else {
```

```
    # Gather the resources using the Gatherer.
            local(@resources) = &GatherResources($database);
            print "<!-- Got resources: @resources -->\n";
            # The query is specified in the command line arguments.
            local($query) = join(' ', @ARGV);
            print "<!-- Got query: @query -->\n";
            # Search the resources using the Search Engine.
            local(@results) = &SearchResources($query, @resources);
            print "<!-- Sorted results are: @results -->\n";
            # Display the top 10 matches.
            print "<!-- Top results are: @results -->\n";
            &DisplaySearchResults($database, @results);
        }
}
# Prints out search results.
# Lists the top-ranking resources first.
# Includes hyperlinks to the full resource content.
sub DisplaySearchResults {
  local($database, @results) = @_;
  local($result, $headline, $score);
  print <<"EndOfSearchResultsHeader";
        <HTML>
        <HEAD><TITLE>SearchGate: Search Results</TITLE></HEAD>
        <BODY>
        <!-- Matched $#results resources in $database database -->
        <H1>SearchGate</H1>
        <H2>Search Results for the <EM>$database</EM> database</H2>
        <P>Please select one of the following:<BR>
        <P>
EndOfSearchResultsHeader
  foreach $result ($results[0..9]) {
            $headline = &GetResourceHeadline($result);
            $score = &GetResourceScore($result);
            $URL = &GetDatabaseResourceURL($database, $result);
            print "<A HREF=\"$URL\">$headline ($score)</A><BR>\n\n";
    }
```

(continued)

169

```
print <<"EndOfSearchResultsFooter";
        </BODY></HTML>
EndOfSearchResultsFooter
}
```

This script uses the **&GatherResources** function in gatherer-lib.pl to collect resources, and the **&SearchResources** function in searcher-lib.pl to search the resources. The **&DisplaySearchResults** function lists the top resources along with a hyperlink to each resource URL.

Utilities for Indexing and Retrieving Resources

This section lists the code for two utility modules used by the resource gatherer and the search engine: the *resource indexer* and the *database retriever.*

The Resource Indexer

Listing 8-4 shows the code for our *resource indexer,* a Perl library called indexer-lib.pl that accepts the index text and title for each resource, and stores these values in the index collection cache for quick access by the search engine. The indexer-lib.pl library provides the following functions:

- **&GetResourceIndex($*resource*)** returns the searchable text index associated with the given resource.

- **&GetResourceHeadline($*resource*)** returns the headline associated with the given resource.

Listing 8-4: The Perl library, indexer-lib.pl, a resource indexer

```
#!/usr/local/bin/perl
# indexer-lib.pl
# Implements a generic resource indexer with a cache for an index
# and a headline.
# The cache consists of these two associative arrays:
%HEADLINES = ();    # Headline text, indexed by resource.
%INDICES = ();      # Resource text, indexed by resource name.
```

```perl
# Returns the index for this resource from the cache.
sub GetResourceIndex {
    local($resource) = @_;
    return($INDICES{$resource});
}
# Gets the headline associated with the given resource.
sub GetResourceHeadline {
  local($resource) = @_;
  return($HEADLINES{$resource});
}
# ---- The internal functions for the indexer ----
# These functions implement indexing over HTML files.
# - The searchable text or "index" is the file with the HTML codes
#    stripped out.
# - The headline is the TITLE of the HTML file or first few
#    characters searchable text.
# Computes and stores the resource index in the cache.
sub StoreResourceIndex{
    local($resource, $index) = @_;
    $index =~ s/<[^>]*>//gi;     # strip out HTML tags
    $index =~ s/\s+/ /g;     # strip out extra whitespace and newlines.
    print "<!-- Index is for $resource is: $index\n -->\n";
    $INDICES{$resource} = $index;
}
# Extract a headline and associate it with the resource.
sub StoreResourceHeadline {
    local($resource, $text, $taggedtext) = @_;
    local($headline) = &GetContentsTitle($taggedtext) ||
                    &GetContentsExcerpt($text);
    print "<!-- Headline for $resource is: $headline\n -->\n";
    $HEADLINES{$resource} = $headline;
    }
# Returns the title of the HTML document (if there is one)
sub GetContentsTitle {
    local($contents) = @_;
    return(&GetElement($contents, 'TITLE'));
}
# Returns an excerpt of the first 20 characters of text.
```

(continued)

```
sub GetContentsExcerpt {
    local($text) = @_;
    return(substr($text, 0, 20)); ;
}
# Returns the contents of a given HTML element.
# Only handles elements that have a matching end tag.
sub GetElement {
    local($doc, $element) = @_;
    if ($doc =~ /<$element>(.*)<\/$element>/) {
    return($1);      # return string between begin & end tags
    }
    else {
    return("");      # no match
    }
}
1; # Always return 1 from libraries
```

The Database Retriever

Listing 8-5 shows a database retriever Perl library, database-lib.pl, that provides quick access to a list of resources, their locations, and their contents. This library provides the following functions:

- **&GetResourceDatabase($*database*)** returns a list of all the resources in the database (by name).

- **&GetDatabaseResourceURL($*database*, $*resource*)** returns the location (URL) for the given resource name in the given database. Used by the search gateway.

- **&GetDatabaseResource($*database*, $*resource*)** returns the entire contents of the given resource.

The search engine, the resource gatherer, and the search gateway all call these functions instead of accessing resources directly.

Listing 8-5: The Perl library, database-lib.pl, a database retriever

```
#!/usr/local/bin/perl
# database-lib.pl
```

```perl
# Implements a database abstraction for retrieving resources.
$DOCROOT = "/etc/httpd"; # Root directory for HTTP server.
# The database is assumed to be a directory on the Web server.
# The resources are retrieved by reading files on the local server
# machine. Only handles a single directory.
# Returns a list of all the resources in the database.
sub GetDatabaseResources {
    local($database) = @_;
    local($file, @files);
    opendir(FILES, &GetDatabaseLocation($database));
    foreach $file (sort readdir(FILES)) {
  if (! -d $file) {        # Don't list directories.
        push(@files, $file);
      }
    }
    return(@files);
}
# Returns a URL for the database entry.
sub GetDatabaseResourceURL {
    local($database, $resource) = @_;
    # Get the SERVER_URL from SERVER_NAME and SERVER_PORT
    $SERVER_URL = "http://" . $ENV{'SERVER_NAME'} .
                        ':' . $ENV{'SERVER_PORT'};
    return("$SERVER_URL/$database/$resource");
}
# Returns the contents of the given resource. A more sophisticated
# version would only return resources less than a given size to keep
# from choking the gatherer on big files.
sub GetDatabaseResource {
    local($database, $resource) = @_;
    local(@lines);
   local($database_loc) = &GetDatabaseLocation($database);
    open(FILE, "$database_loc/$resource");
    @lines = <FILE>;     # Read in the whole file.
    # Close the file.
    close(FILE);
    # Change all newlines to spaces.
    return join(' ', @lines);
}
```

(continued)

173

```
# ---- Internal functions for the database retriever ----
# Returns the location of the database.
# If the server supports the DOCUMENT_ROOT environment var, uses it.
sub GetDatabaseLocation {
    local($database) = @_;
    local($location) = $ENV{'DOCUMENT_ROOT'} || $DOCROOT;
    print "<!-- The $database DB is at $location/$database -->\n";
    return("$location/$database");
}
1; # always return 1 from libraries
```

How to Install and Use the Search Gateway

To use the SearchGate search gateway, you must install the search facility code, create one or more databases, and run the CGI script searchgate.pl.

Installing the Code

To install the search facility code, follow these steps:

1. Copy the files gatherer-lib.pl, searcher-lib.pl, database-lib.pl, indexer-lib.pl, and searchgate.pl to your executable CGI script directory. On our server, this is /etc/httpd/cgi-bin.

2. Open the database-lib.pl file and set the $DOCROOT variable to the complete path to where your HTML files are stored.

3. Create a /responses directory to hold error documents. Locate it as a "sister" directory to /cgi-bin(/etc/httpd/responses).

4. Create an error document called searchgate_err_no_database. html. If no database is supplied, the search gateway will print this document.

Creating Databases

To use the search facility, you must create one or more databases. Do the following:

1. Create a "database" directory on your Web server machine to hold your resource files. This directory should be created under the document directory that you specified during your Web server installation. For example, if your document directory is /etc/httpd and your database is Internet, in UNIX you would do the following:

```
$ mkdir /etc/httpd/Internet
```

2. Set up a collection of HTML documents in the database directory. Here is a sample HTML file you might want to use:

```
<HTML>
<HEAD>
<TITLE> Internet Search Engines </TITLE>
</HEAD>
<BODY>
Document describing various finding facilities on the Net.
</BODY>
</HTML>
```

Using the Search Gateway

To run the search gateway, access the CGI URL for searchgate.pl and supply the name of the database directory in the path information. For example, to search the Internet database, use the URL

```
http://www.yourserver.com/cgi-bin/searchgate.pl/Internet".
```

If you enter keywords into the search field, as in "Internet search engines," you should see a Web page like that shown in Figure 8-9.

Now that you understand the basics of search gateways, you can extend SearchGate to fit your particular needs.

As you come to the end of Part II, you have learned all of the major components of a good Web information service: dynamic Web pages, interactive forms with informative responses, and search gateways. In Part III, you'll see it all put together in a catalog-shopping service application for the Web.

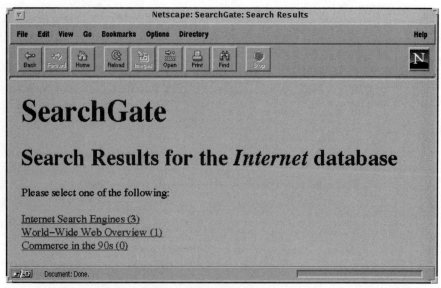

Figure 8-9: Output from the searchgate.pl search gateway

Part **Three**

Applications and Future Developments

In the first part of this book you studied some useful programming techniques — now it's time to put them to work. We'll start by taking a look at how to gather requirements and design applications for the Web (Chapter 9). Along the way, we'll create a complete design for a Web-based shopping service application. In Chapter 10, you'll see how to implement this shopping service using Perl 5. You can use this sample application to get jump-started on projects of your own.

Chapter 11 offers suggestions and cautions about security. You'll find out how to protect your Web server, your company, and your data, as well as your users' on-line transactions, from hackers operating over the Internet.

In Chapter 12, you'll find information about new languages and toolkits for creating Web-based applications — plus new ways of doing business. Then in Chapter 13, we give you a resource guide that tells you where to go to start learning more about creating CGI programs and implementing them in Perl.

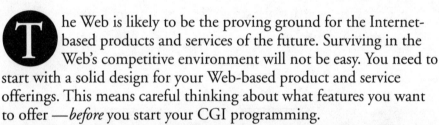

Chapter 9

Designing an Application for the Web

T he Web is likely to be the proving ground for the Internet-based products and services of the future. Surviving in the Web's competitive environment will not be easy. You need to start with a solid design for your Web-based product and service offerings. This means careful thinking about what features you want to offer —*before* you start your CGI programming.

This chapter gives you valuable information and examples for how to design your features for users surfing the Web. You'll learn how to break down your idea into small software components, map out the flow of information between these components, organize the necessary data, and plan your implementation.

To demonstrate the concepts of Web application design, we'll design a simple application: an on-line catalog shopping service. Then, in Chapter 10, Implementing a Complete CGI Application, we'll implement the service using Perl 5.

Decide on a Good List of Features

When designing your information service or application, first list some of the features you would like to offer. You should be as detailed as possible about the requirements for these features. For example, our shopping service will provide these two major features:

179

- *Browsing:* Moving through product catalogs, a Web page at a time.
- *Ordering:* Selecting products and ordering them by e-mail.

Create a Task/Action Diagram

The next step in the design is to think about how people will utilize your information service. Where will they start? How many steps does it take to carry out important tasks? How many choices do users have at every step of the way? To answer these questions, it's best to construct a *task/action diagram.* This diagram shows major tasks performed by the user and the actions that transition the user between these tasks.

Figure 9-1 shows the task/action diagram for our shopping service. The major tasks are

- Choosing from a list of catalogs (Storefront Shop)
- Browsing a particular catalog (Browse Catalog)
- Ordering products from a catalog (Order Products)

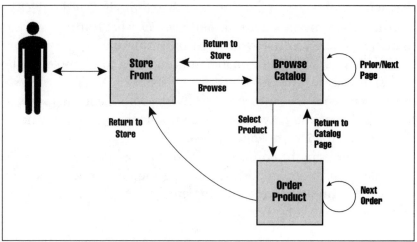

Figure 9-1: Task/action diagram for shopping service application

Large tasks can be broken down into smaller subtasks. For example, ordering products requires two subtasks:

- Confirming product selections
- Confirming billing data

The actions possible from the Browse Catalog task are

- Moving to the previous product in the catalog (Prior)
- Moving to the next product in the catalog (Next)
- Selecting a product to order (Select Product)
- Selecting another catalog (Return to Store)

Guidelines for Task/Action Diagram

Follow these guidelines when you're producing a task/action diagram for Web-based software:

- Provide a simple and consistent way for users to navigate among your Web pages.
- Offer at least one "path of least resistance." Never leave a user stranded with no available hyperlinks.
- Give users quick access to the features that are most important and most used.
- Whenever you return users to a previous Web page, return them to that page in the state it was in when they left it.

Step Users Through The Process

After you're done with your diagram, the next step is to carefully watch a potential visitor to your site as they try each action. Walk through a realistic scenario, using the task/action diagram as a guide for what your application should do. If a user can't figure out where they are in the process, how they got there, or what they should be doing, it's time to rework your design.

Design and Prototype the User Interface

After you have an idea of how your application will be used, it's time to create a high-level interface design and prototype. Decide on an overall metaphor or theme (a highway or desktop, for instance). Choose the media you want to use—formatted text, postscript or PDF files, thumbnail graphics, audio or video clips, 3-D environment, animations, and so on. Also, figure out how to lay out those media on the page, perhaps in newspaper columns or horizontal sections.

Figure 9-2 shows the Web page design for our shopping service. The arrows depict the most likely path of the user through the service. Laying out all of your pages in this fashion helps you get the "big picture," and helps you spot inconsistencies and missing pieces in your design.

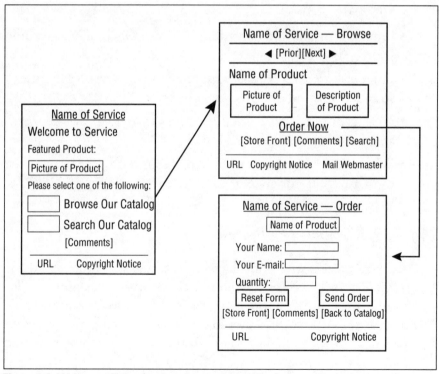

Figure 9-2: Web page design for shopping service application

Guidelines for Interface Design

Here are some general guidelines for creating good Web designs:

- Target people who are new to your service, and then add features for more experienced users.

- Keep your Web pages small and somewhat self-contained.

- At each step, tell users what to expect next.

- Don't make your Web pages look like paper documents. Web pages can be *interactive*.

- Engage the user with your program, and users with one another. Web pages can permit *collaboration*.

Break It Down into Software Components

The *software component design* assigns software components to the various features of the system. We distinguish the following types of components:

- *Modules:* Parts of CGI programs that perform specific functions

- *Scripts:* Individual CGI programs that generate a single dynamic Web page

- *Facilities:* One or more CGI programs that work together

Our shopping service consists of the following components:

- *Storefront Script:* Generates a home page with a list of catalogs.

- *Browsing Script:* Displays product description pages from a database, page by page. Selecting the picture of a product will order the product by calling the order form script with that product name.

- *Ordering Facility:* Displays an order form for the product and sends the completed order to the order processing department via e-mail.

The ordering facility consists of two scripts:

- *Product Selection Script:* Displays a list of products in the catalog. The product that the user was last browsing is automatically selected. Users can select more products and then submit their order.

- *Billing Script:* Provides a total bill. Prompts for user identity (name and e-mail address) and billing information. In our implementation, we leave off the billing information.

It's best to design your software starting with entire facilities and working down to the level of modules.

Specify the Data Flow

You also need to specify which data needs to be passed among programs or modules. You can do this with a *data flow diagram* that shows software components and the flow of various data elements among them.

Figure 9-3 shows the data flow diagram for our Web-based shopping service. You can easily see from this diagram that the current catalog and selected product need to be passed among the storefront script, browsing script, and order form script.

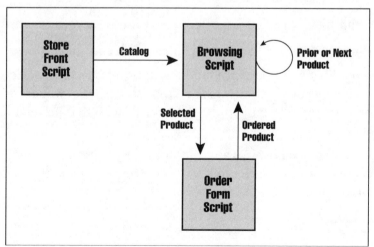

Figure 9-3: Data flow diagram for the shopping service

Tip: Remember that HTTP is *stateless,* so context information (such as the user's "location" within the service) cannot easily be "remembered" by a CGI program between invocations. You must decide on all of the information that each script needs and specify it in the diagram. When you write your CGI programs, this information will likely appear in CGI URLs.

Provide a Data Map

Next, decide on how you are going to organize your data. Create a *data map* showing the breakdown of data into various parts and subparts. If you plan to use Perl 5 to implement your application, try to employ an object-oriented methodology to create your data map. You'll need to define object classes, individual object instances, attributes, and values.

Figure 9-4 shows the data map for our Web-based shopping service.

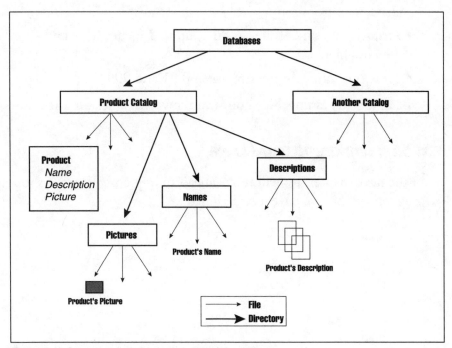

Figure 9-4: Data map for Web-based shopping service

The two main classes of objects for the shopping service application are as follows:

- *Catalogs:* A collection of products that can be browsed together (a list of software products, for instance)
- *Products:* Items that can be purchased, which have attributes such as name, description, and price

Products

Each of the products is a single object instance, with an identical set of attributes:

- *Name:* The name of the product, up to 30 characters.
- *Catalog:* The catalog where this product is listed; each product can appear in only one catalog.
- *Description:* A formatted description of the product, up to 300 characters.
- *Picture:* A picture of the product, up to 2 inches wide and 3 inches high.
- *Price:* A decimal number between 0.01 and 999.99.

Be as specific as possible about the allowable values for attributes.

Next Step: Implement Your Design

In the next chapter, we will move ahead to implementing the shopping service that we have just designed.

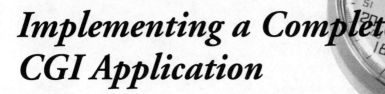

## Chapter 10

Implementing a Complete CGI Application

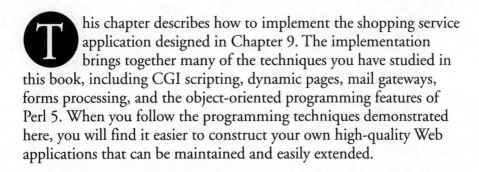

T his chapter describes how to implement the shopping service application designed in Chapter 9. The implementation brings together many of the techniques you have studied in this book, including CGI scripting, dynamic pages, mail gateways, forms processing, and the object-oriented programming features of Perl 5. When you follow the programming techniques demonstrated here, you will find it easier to construct your own high-quality Web applications that can be maintained and easily extended.

Web Pages for the Shopping Service

The shopping service application provides a way for users to order products over the Web. It consists of a storefront, a product catalog, and an ordering facility.

The Storefront

The storefront, which displays a list of product catalogs, is the first Web page that users see when they access the shopping service. Figure 10-1 shows a sample storefront with hyperlinks to two catalogs: a Tools catalog and a Software catalog.

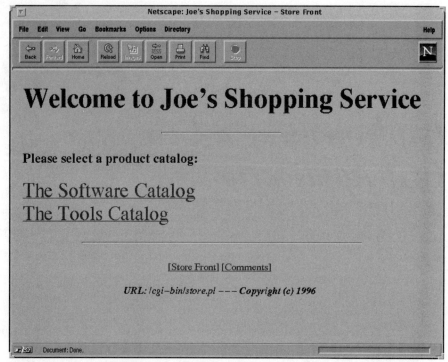

Figure 10-1: The Joe's Shopping Service storefront page with two product catalogs

The page footer appears at the bottom of every major Web page of our shopping service. As shown in Figure 10-1, the first line of the footer consists of the hyperlinks [Store Front] and [Comments]. Selecting the [Comments] hyperlink leads to the Comments facility that we completed in Chapter 7. Selecting [Storefront] moves the user back to the Storefront page.

The Catalog Pages

When the user selects the hyperlink for a given catalog, the service opens up that catalog to the first page. For example, the hyperlink for The Software Catalog displays the page shown in Figure 10-2.

The user can page forward and backward through the catalog using the [<=Previous Page] and [Next Page=>] hyperlinks. At any time, the ordering facility can be accessed by clicking on either the displayed picture of the product or the Order Now! hyperlink.

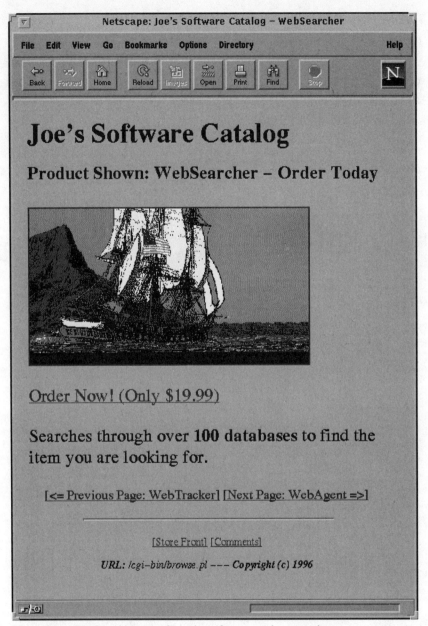

Figure 10-2: The first Web page from the software products catalog

The Ordering Facility

The ordering facility consists of a product selection form and a billing form.

The Product Selection Form

The product selection form allows users to buy products from the catalog they are browsing. All products are listed, and the product last seen by the user is automatically selected. Users can then select additional products to buy, as shown in Figure 10-3.

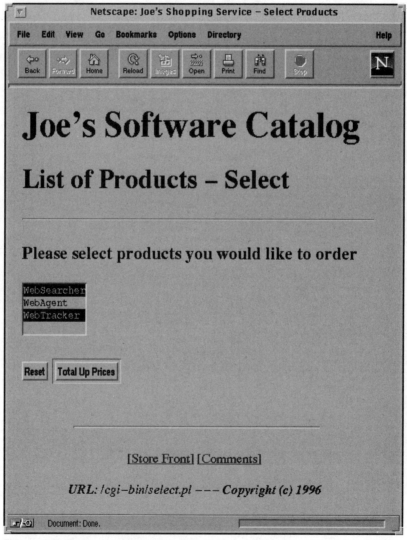

Figure 10-3: The product selection form

When the user submits the product selection form, the shopping service automatically totals the order and generates a billing form.

The Billing Form

The billing form, shown in Figure 10-4, lists the products that the user selected and the total price. If this were a real billing form, it would also request payment information, such as a credit card number. Our form just asks users for their name and e-mail address.

Figure 10-4: A sample billing form

When the user submits the billing form, a CGI script validates the information provided. Our script checks to make sure that the user has provided a name and e-mail address. If everything is okay, the completed order is displayed, as shown in Figure 10-5. The completed order is automatically e-mailed to an order processing department.

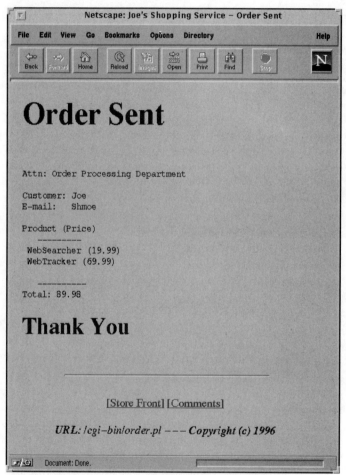

Figure 10-5: A confirmation message after a successful order

You can find the code for this application at

```
http://www.idgbooks.com/idgbooksonline/CGI
```

Before we look at the page templates and CGI scripts needed to produce each of these Web pages, let's create a sample product database that we can use to test our service.

Creating the Product Database

Each product catalog offered by the shopping service describes a number of products stored in a database. All of the information about the products is in this database or various auxiliary files. Included are the product's name, a description, a picture, the cost, and the name of the catalog to which the product belongs.

We will first create the necessary directories to hold product-related files, and then fill these directories with sample files. When we are done, we will have a complete product database.

Directories for the Product Data

There are three kinds of product-related files: product object files, description files, and picture files. First, let's create a directory to hold product object files.

1. Move to your Web server's document root directory. For example, at our UNIX installation, we would enter

```
$ cd /etc/httpd
```

2. Create a directory named Objects. In UNIX, you can enter

```
$ mkdir Objects
```

3. Next, we need to create directories to hold the pictures of products and their formatted descriptions. Make a directory named Picture to store the GIF files for the picture attribute:

```
$ mkdir Picture
```

4. Create a directory named Description to hold the HTML files for the description attribute:

```
$ mkdir Description
```

The other product data — name, catalog, and price — are stored directly in the product object file. Table 10-1 lists each product attribute and the proper format for its value.

Now that that we know where product data goes and its proper format, we are ready to create a sample database for the shopping service. Let's start with product object files.

Table 10-1: Product Attribute Value Formats

ATTRIBUTE NAME	PROPER FORMAT FOR ITS VALUE
name	Text string (<300 char)
catalog	Text string (<300 char)
description	Name of HTML file (8 char + .html)
picture	Name of GIF file (8 char + .gif)
price	Decimal number (0.01 to 9999.99)

Product Object Files

To create a new product object file, use a text editor such as Notepad on Windows or **emacs** on UNIX. Each attribute of the product is stored on a separate line in this file. Enter the name of the attribute (price, for instance), followed by one or more spaces, followed by the value. Here is a sample file for a product called WebSearcher:

```
name WebSearcher
catalog Software
description searcher.html
picture searcher.gif
price 19.99
```

Save the product object file in the Objects directory and make sure it has the filename extension .obj. The full path for this file on our UNIX system is

```
/etc/httpd/Objects/searcher.obj
```

About Product IDs

All products must have unique IDs. The file's name without its .obj extension is the product ID. For example, in the WebSearcher file just above, the product ID for WebSearcher is *searcher*.

Note: Your Web server daemon must have permission to read your product data directories and files. If you are on a UNIX platform, you can give everyone read access to these files using the **chmod** command. For example, the command

```
chmod ugo+r *.obj
```

gives everyone read access to all filenames ending in .obj.

Product Description Files

Next, you have to create a product description file. All product description files are HTML files stored in the Description directory.

Here is a sample product description for the WebSearcher product:

```
Searches through over <STRONG>100 databases</STRONG> to find the
item you are looking for.
```

Save the product description file you've just made as *searcher.html*. On our UNIX machine, the complete directory path to this file is

```
/etc/httpd/Description/searcher.html
```

The name of a description file should always be the product ID followed by the filename extension .html.

Product Picture Files

Now let's see how to store the pictures associated with each product. In Figure 10-2, the picture of the product is a sailing ship. All pictures are stored as GIF files in the /pictures directory.

Note: Depending on your browser's capabilities, you may be able to use a different image format, such as JPEG or PNG.

Use the product ID as the filename, with a .gif extension. Our complete directory path to the picture of the WebSearcher product is

```
/etc/httpd/Picture/searcher.gif
```

Filling Out the Database

Now that you know how to add products to the database, let's fill out the database a bit.

Let's add two more products, WebTracker and WebAgent, to the Software catalog. After you add their auxiliary files, your Software catalog database should look like that shown in Table 10-2.

For testing purposes, you should create another entire catalog named Tools with three more products of your choice. When you are done creating these directories and files, you will have a sample product database sufficient for testing your CGI scripts.

Table 10-2: Summary of Database for Software Catalog Installation

FILE TYPE	PRODUCT	DIRECTORY/FILE
Product Info (plain text)	WebSearcher	/Objects/searcher.obj
	WebTracker	/Objects/tracker.obj
	WebAgent	/Objects/agent.obj
Pictures (GIF)	WebSearcher	/Picture/searcher.gif
	WebTracker	/Picture/tracker.gif
	WebAgent	/Picture/agent.gif
Descriptions (HTML)	WebSearcher	/Description/searcher.html
	WebTracker	/Description/tracker.html
	WebAgent	/Description/agent.html

The Product Catalog Perl Library

Listing 10-1 gives the code for catalog-lib.pl, a Perl 5.0 library that gives our CGI scripts access to catalogs and products. Save this file as catalog-lib.pl and put it in the cgi-libs subdirectory under your CGI script directory. On our UNIX server, the complete path is

```
/etc/httpd/cgi-bin/cgi-libs/catalog-lib.pl
```

This library provides the following functions:

- **&GetCatalogs()** returns a list of all the catalog names, sorted alphabetically.
- **&SetCatalog($catalog)** sets the current catalog to $catalog.
- **&GetProducts($catalog)** returns a list of all the products in the given catalog, $catalog, sorted alphabetically.
- **&GetProduct($productID)** returns the product with the given product ID, $productID.
- **&GetProductByName($name)** returns the product with the given name, $name.
- **&GetProduct_Info($product)** returns all known information about the given product, $product, in an associative array.
- **&GetFirstProduct()** returns the first product in the current catalog.

196

- **&GetPreviousProduct(*$product*)** returns the product just before *$product* in the current catalog, or an empty string ('') if *$product* is the first product.

- **&GetNextProduct($*product*)** returns the product just after *$product* in the current catalog, or an empty string ('') if *$product* is the last product.

Tip: It is a good practice to list the functions that you use from various libraries, along with their arguments, as we have done in the code listings in this chapter.

Listing 10-1: catalog-lib.pl, a Perl 5 library for accessing catalogs of products

```perl
#!/usr/local/bin/perl5
# catalog-lib.pl
# Manages catalogs of product objects.

require 'object-lib.pl';  # Uses the persistent object library

package Catalog;          # All functions are in this package.

%PRODUCTS = ();           # A list of all product objects in
                          # the current catalog, keyed by name.


# --- Functions provided ---
# Returns a list of all the catalogs. Each catalog is just a string.
sub GetCatalogs {
   local($catalog, $product, %catalogs) = ();
   local(@allproducts) = &Object::GetAllObjects();
   foreach $product (@allproducts) {
     $catalog = &Object::Get_Value($product,'catalog');
     $catalogs{$catalog} = 1; # Mark this catalog
   }
   return(sort keys %catalogs); # Now returned the marked catalogs.
}
```

(continued)

```
# Sets the current catalog to $catalog.
# All subsequent calls to functions will assume products in
# this catalog.
# Returns a list of products.
sub SetCatalog {
    local($catalog) = @_;
    local($product, $prodcatalog, $prodname);
    %PRODUCTS = ();
    @allproducts = &Object::GetAllObjects();
    foreach $product (@allproducts) {
      $prodcatalog = &Object::Get_Value($product, 'catalog');
      if ($prodcatalog eq $catalog) {
    $prodname = &Object::Get_Value($product, 'name');
    $PRODUCTS{$prodname} = $product;
      }
    }
    return(values %PRODUCTS);
}


# Must be called after SetCatalog.
sub GetProducts {
    return(sort values %PRODUCTS);
}


# Get the product object for this ID.
sub GetProduct {
    local($productID) = @_;
    local($product) = &Object::GetObject($productID);
    return($product);
}


# Using an associative array, keyed by name,
# makes this lookup easy.
sub GetProductByName {
    local($name) = @_;
    return($PRODUCTS{$name});
}
```

```perl
# Returns all product info in an associative array, including
# description (a "persistent" attribute because its value is in
# a file that is read in), name, catalog, picture, and price.
sub GetProduct_Info {
    local($product) = @_;
    # Description is the only attribute stored in an include file.
    local(%info) = &Object::Read($product, 'description',
                          ('name', 'catalog', 'picture', 'price'));
    return(%info);
}


# We must use the method Get_Value in this function
# because object information is read "on demand".
sub GetProduct_Name {
    local($product) = @_;
    local($name) = &Object::Get_Value($product, 'name');
    return($name);
}


# Also uses the Get_Value method. Setting a local variable,
# then returning it like we have done with $name,
# allows you to insert a line to print out its value before
# you return it.
sub GetProduct_Price {
    local($product) = @_;
    local($name) = &Object::Get_Value($product, 'price');
    return($name);
}


# Returns the first product in the catalog. Remember that
# array indices start at zero ( 0 ).
sub GetFirstProduct {
  return((sort values %PRODUCTS)[0]);
}
```

(continued)

```
# Returns the product immediately prior to the one given,
# or an empty string if the given product is the first.
sub GetPreviousProduct {
    local($product) = @_;
    local(@products) = values(%PRODUCTS); # list all products
    local($ID) = $product->{'ID'};
    local($i) =  &getCatalogPosition($ID, @products);
    if ($i <= 0) {
        return('');
     }
   else {
   local($prev) = $products[$i - 1]; # get previous product
   return($prev);
     }
}


# Returns the product immediately after the one given,
# or an empty string if the given product is the last.
sub GetNextProduct {
    local($product) = @_;
    local(@products) = values(%PRODUCTS);
    local($ID) = $product->{'ID'};
    local($i) =  &getCatalogPosition($ID, @products);
    if ($i >= $#products) {
        return('');
     }
   else {
   local($next) = $products[$i + 1]; # get the next product
   return($next);
     }
}


# --- Utility functions ---
# Returns the position of $ID in the list of
# products, @products. -1 if not found.
sub getCatalogPosition {
```

```
    local($ID, @products) = @_;
    for($i=0;$i <= $#products;$i++) { # loop over all subscripts
  if ($ID eq $products[$i]->{'ID'}) { # if the ID matches, then
      return($i);                       # return the array subscript
  }
  }
  return(-1); # not found
}


1; # always return 1 (true) from libraries
```

Required Files, Scripts, and Libraries

The catalog-lib.pl library creates and manipulates Perl 5.0 objects for each product. However, instead of creating a special object class (package) for our product objects, we will instead create a general Perl library that manipulates objects in an object class called Object. The source code for object-lib.pl is listed at the end of this chapter.

The Storefront

The storefront page for the shopping service application provides a list of product catalogs that the user can access. This section describes the template for the storefront and the CGI script that fills in this template. The resulting page will look something like Figure 10-1.

The Storefront Page Template

Listing 10-2 gives the HTML codes for the storefront page template, store.html. Save this file in your templates directory. The complete path on our UNIX server is

```
/etc/httpd/templates/store.html
```

The following variables are used in the store.html page template:

- *!!menu!!* lists hyperlinks to each of the available catalogs.
- *!!footer!!* lists the CGI URL for the script that filled in this page template, plus a copyright notice.

Listing 10-2: store.html, the template for our shopping service storefront page

```
<HTML>
<HEAD><TITLE>Joe's Shopping Service - Storefront</TITLE></HEAD>
<BODY><H1>Welcome to Joe's Shopping Service</H1>
<HR SIZE=3 WIDTH=30%>
<H3>Please select a product catalog:</H3><FONT SIZE=5>
!!menu!!
</FONT><BR><HR SIZE=3 WIDTH=70%><BR>
!!footer!!
</BODY>
</HTML>
```

Note: Not all Web browsers accept the SIZE and WIDTH attributes for <HR> and the <FONT> element used in Listing 10-2. If your browser does not accept these attributes, it will skip over them.

The CGI Script for the Storefront

Listing 10-3 gives the CGI script that displays the storefront page. Save this CGI script as store.pl and move it to your CGI script directory. The complete path on our UNIX server is

```
/etc/httpd/cgi-bin/store.pl
```

Listing 10-3: store.pl, the CGI script for the shopping service storefront page

```
#!/usr/local/bin/perl5
# store.pl
# Displays the storefront page.
push(@INC, 'cgi-libs');
require 'templates-lib.pl';
    # Uses FillTemplateFile($template, %var_values)
require 'catalog-lib.pl';
    # Uses GetCatalogs($catalog);
require 'footer-lib.pl';
```

```perl
   # Uses GetFooter($template);
MAIN: {
   # Initialize associative array for filling in templates.
   local(%vars) = ();
   # Add CGI header;
   print "Content-type: text/html\n\n";
   # Get menu of catalogs and footer & add them to %vars.
   $vars{'menu'} = &getCatalogMenu();
   $vars{'footer'} = &Footer::GetFooter();
   # Replace the template variables in the page template & print;
   print &Templates::FillTemplateFile("../templates/store.html",
%vars);
}
# --- Utility functions ---
# Create a menu of hyperlinks to catalogs.
sub getCatalogMenu {
   local($doc) = '';
   local(@catalogs) = &Catalog::GetCatalogs();
  # Note that we use form-like URLs in your hyperlinks.
  # This leaves  PATH_INFO free for tracing information.
   foreach $catalog (@catalogs) {
     $doc .= "<A HREF=\"/cgi-bin/browse.pl?catalog=$catalog\">The
$catalog Catalog</A><BR>";
  }
   # Returns the accumulated document.
   return($doc);
  }
  }
```

Tip: To require a Perl code library without giving a long directory path, use the @INC array. For example, if all of your code libraries come from the /cgi-libs directory, just add this line before you **require** them:

```perl
push(@INC, 'cgi-libs');
```

This line will **push** the cgi-libs directory onto the end of the predefined Perl array named @INC. The Perl interpreter looks through all of the directories on the @INC list when loading required files.

Files, Scripts, and Libraries

This section explains the page templates, CGI scripts, and Perl libraries you need for the storefront.

The Page Templates Library

The store.pl script uses templates-lib.pl (Listing 5-1 in Chapter 5), so be sure this Perl library is installed in your /cgi-libs directory before running the storefront script. On our UNIX server, the complete path to the templates library is

```
/etc/httpd/cgi-bin/cgi-libs/templates-lib.pl
```

The Page Footer Template

Listing 10-4 gives the page template we use to generate the page footers for the shopping service application, including the footer used in the storefront page template, store.html. Save this file as footer.html in your templates directory. On our UNIX server, the complete path is

```
/etc/httpd/templates/footer.html
```

Take notice of the following features in footer.html:

* The hyperlink to the store.pl CGI script brings users back to the storefront page. This is helpful when they want to quit browsing or cancel their order and start over at the setorefront page.

* The hyperlink to the comments.pl CGI script calls the Comments facility (Listing 7-4). This allows users to give feedback to the Webmaster at the very moment they are having difficulty.

* The <ADDRESS> element only uses one template variable: !!SCRIPT_NAME!!, the relative path to the script that generated the current page.

Listing 10-4: footer.html, the generic page footer for our shopping service application

```
<CENTER>
<A HREF="/cgi-bin/store.pl">[Storefront]</A>
<A HREF="/cgi-bin/comments.pl">[Comments]</A>
<P><ADDRESS>
<STRONG>URL: </STRONG>!!SCRIPT_NAME!! --
```

```
<STRONG>Copyright (c) 1996</STRONG>
</ADDRESS>
</CENTER>
```

Note: This template and many others in this chapter include HTML tags that are either Netscape extensions or part of the HTML/3.0 draft proposal. For example, the <CENTER> tag is a Netscape extension that centers the enclosed items on the Web page. (If your browser doesn't recognize one of these special tags, it will ignore it.)

The footer-lib.pl CGI Script

Listing 10-5 gives a Perl library we use to generate footers for all of our shopping service Web pages. Save this file to footer-lib.pl and place it in the /cgi-libs subdirectory under your CGI script executables directory. Our path is

```
/etc/httpd/cgi-bin/cgi-libs/footer-lib.pl
```

This library provides the function **GetFooter(*$template*)**, which fills in the footer insert template, *$template*. It substitutes the values of any CGI environment variables that appear as template variables. (SERVER_NAME appears as !!SERVER_NAME!!, for instance.) This function uses footer.html if no template is given as its argument.

Listing 10-5: footer-lib.pl, a Perl library to generate Web page footers

```
#!/usr/local/bin/perl5
# footer-lib.pl
# Computes a page footer using a footer template.
package Footer;
require 'templates-lib.pl';
   # Uses: &FillTemplateFile($template_file, %var_values);
# --- Functions provided: ---
# Fills in whatever footer template is in the templates directory or
# is passed as an arguments. Assumes only CGI env vars in %ENV used.
sub GetFooter {
   local($template) = @_;
```

(continued)

```
    $template = "footer.html" unless $template;
    return(&Templates::FillTemplateFile("../templates/$template", %ENV));
}
1; # Always return 1 (true) from libraries
```

The Comments Form and comments.pl CGI Script

Make sure that comments.html (Listing 6-1) is installed in your Web server's document root directory. On our machine, the complete path is

```
/etc/httpd/comments.html
```

Also make sure that comments.pl (see Listing 6-3) is installed in your CGI script executables directory. On our machine, the complete path is

```
/etc/httpd/cgi-bin/comments.pl
```

In addition, comments_confirm.html (Listing 7-2) should be installed in your /responses directory:

```
/etc/httpd/responses/comments_confirm.html
```

The error document, comments_err_no_addr.html (Listing 7-3), should be installed in the /responses directory, as well:

```
/etc/httpd/responses/comments_err_no_addr.html
```

The Catalog Browsing Feature

The browsing feature of our shopping service allows the user to move forward and backward through an individual catalog, page by page. When the desired item is located, it can be ordered by selecting it. This section describes the page template and CGI script needed to implement these features.

The Catalog Page Template

Listing 10-6 shows the page template we will use to generate each of the pages in our product catalogs. Save this file as browse.html in your /templates directory. Our path is

```
/etc/httpd/templates/browse.html
```

The following variables are used in this page template:

- **!!product!!** is the product ID for the selected product.

- **!!name!!**, **!!catalog!!**, **!!price!!**, **!!picture!!**, and **!!description!!** are the values of the attributes of this product.

- **!!controls!!** lists the hyperlinks to previous and next catalog pages.

- **!!footer!!** is the generic page footer.

Listing 10-6: browse.html, the product catalog page template for our shopping service

```
<HTML>
<HEAD><TITLE>Joe's !!catalog!! Catalog - !!name!!</TITLE></HEAD>
<BODY><H1>Joe's !!catalog!! Catalog </H1>
<H2> Product Shown: !!name!! - Order Today</H2><BR><FONT SIZE=5>
<A HREF=
    "/cgi-bin/select.pl?catalog=!!catalog!!&product=!!product!!">
    <IMG SRC="/picture/!!picture!!"><BR>
    <P>Order Now! (Only $!!price!!)<BR>
</A><BR>
!!description!!
<BR><BR></FONT><FONT SIZE=4>
<CENTER>
!!controls!!
</CENTER></FONT><BR><HR SIZE=3 WIDTH=70%><BR>
!!footer!!
</BODY>
</HTML>
```

The Catalog Browsing CGI Script

Listing 10-7 gives the Perl CGI script that implements the catalog browsing feature. Save this CGI script as browse.pl and move it to your CGI script directory. Our complete path is

```
/etc/httpd/cgi-bin/browse.pl
```

Here are a couple of things to note about browse.pl:

- This script prints the Content-type header first and then uses HTML comments to provide debugging information, as recommended in Chapter 4.

- The same script is used when a product *has* been selected as when one has *not* been selected. This makes the implementation simpler and more compact.

Listing 10-7: browse.pl, the CGI script that generates the product catalog pages

```perl
#!/usr/local/bin/perl5
# browse.pl
# Displays a page in a product catalog.
push(@INC, "cgi-libs");
require 'templates-lib.pl';
   # Uses FillTemplateFile($template, %var_values)
require 'forms-lib.pl';
   # Uses GetFormInput();
require 'catalog-lib.pl';
   # Uses SetCatalog($catalog)
   #      GetProduct($productID);
   #      GetFirstProduct();
   #      GetProduct_Info($product);
   #      GetProduct_Name($product);
   #      GetPreviousProduct($product);
   #      GetNextProduct($product);
require 'footer-lib.pl';
   # Uses GetFooter($template);
MAIN: {
    # Declare local variables;
    local($product);
    # Add Content-type CGI header;
    print "Content-type: text/html\n\n";
    # Extract information from the URL:
    local(%input) = &GetFormInput();
    local($catalog) = $input{'catalog'};
    print "<!-- Got catalog: $catalog -->\n";
    &Catalog::SetCatalog($catalog);
```

```perl
    local($productID) = $input{'product'};
    # If the user is paging through, we have a product ID. Just
    # get the corresponding object.
    if ($productID) {
        $product = &Catalog::GetProduct($productID);
    }
    # Otherwise, get first product. else {
        $product = &Catalog::GetFirstProduct();
    }
    print "<!-- Product ID is: [$product->{'ID'}] -->\n";
    # Get variables for filling in template.
    local(%vars) = &Catalog::GetProduct_Info($product);
    local($prev) = &Catalog::GetPreviousProduct($product);
    print "<!-- Previous catalog item is: $prev->{'ID'} -->\n";
    local($next) = &Catalog::GetNextProduct($product);
    print "<!-- Next catalog item is: $next->{'ID'} -->\n";
    $vars{'product'} = $product->{'ID'};
    $vars{'controls'} = &getLinks($catalog, $prev, $next);
    $vars{'footer'} = &Footer::GetFooter();
      # Replace the template variables in the page template & print.
    print &Templates::FillTemplateFile("../templates/browse.html",
                              %vars);
}
# -- Utility functions --
# Generates hyperlinks to previous and next products in the catalog.
sub getLinks {
    local($catalog, $prev, $next) = @_;
  # If no surrounding objects, return immediately.
  if ($prev eq '' && $next eq '') {
        return('');
  }
  else {
    # Initialize the return string.
    local($doc) = '';
    # If there previous page exists, call browse.pl w/ proper ID.
     if ($prev) {
        local($prevID) = $prev->{'ID'};
```

(continued)

```
        local($prevname) = &Catalog::GetProduct_Name($prev);
        $doc .= "<A
    HREF=\"/cgi-bin/browse.pl?catalog=$catalog&product=$prevID\">
        [<= Previous Page: $prevname]</A>\n";
      }
    # If there is a next page, do the same.
    if ($next) {
        local($nextID) =  $next->{'ID'};
        local($nextname) =  &Catalog::GetProduct_Name($next);
        $doc .= "<A
    HREF=\"/cgi-bin/browse.pl?catalog=$catalog&product=$nextID\">
        [Next Page: $nextname =>]</A>\n";
      }
    }
   # Return the accumulated string.
   return($doc);
}
```

Required Files, Scripts, and Libraries

The browser.pl script uses forms-lib.pl (Listing 6-2 in Chapter 6) to get
the name of the catalog and optional product ID. Make sure forms-
lib.pl is in the /cgi-libs subdirectory before you execute browser.pl. On
our UNIX machine, the complete path to forms-lib.pl is

```
/etc/httpd/cgi-bin/cgi-libs/forms-lib.pl
```

The browser.pl script also uses catalog-lib.pl, templates-lib.pl, and
footer-lib.pl, all of which should already be installed in your cgi-libs
directory.

The Ordering Feature

The ordering facility allows the user to place orders for products via e-
mail. This section gives the templates and forms for both the product
selection form and the billing form.

The Product Selection Form

The select.pl CGI script generates the product selection form (Figure 10-3) by filling in the page template, select.html. Let's look at the page template first.

Template for the Product Selection Page

Listing 10-8 gives the HTML codes for select.html, the product selection page template. Save this file in your templates directory. The complete path on our UNIX server is

```
/etc/httpd/templates/select.html
```

There are several things to note about this HTML template:

- The name of the catalog is automatically passed on to billing.pl. An <INPUT> element of type HIDDEN sets the value of the catalog, as if the user had typed it in directly. This value is then passed to the CGI program that processes the form — in this case, billing.pl. Because the field is hidden, it will not appear on the Web page.

- More than one product can be selected. The products are listed with a <SELECT> element having a MULTIPLE attribute. The SIZE attribute limits the size of the list to four items; more than four will introduce a scroll bar.

- The products selected will be passed on to the billing.pl script using the "products" attribute ("products" is the NAME of the <SELECT> attribute). If multiple products are selected, the "products" attribute will appear multiple times in the URL that calls billing.pl. Thus, if the user selects WebSearcher and WebTracker, the resulting CGI URL would be

```
/cgi-bin/billing.pl?products=WebSearcher&products=WebTracker
```

The select.html page template uses the following template variables:

- **!!option!!** is a string containing all of the <OPTION> elements, one for each product. Each <OPTION> element displays the product's name and price and lets the user select the product using a toggle (on-off) button. More than one toggle can be selected, but the product selection CGI script will generate an error if none are selected.

211

- **!!footer!!** is a string containing the generic page footer, after all template variable substitutions have been made using &Footer::GetFooter.

Listing 10-8: select.html, the product selection page template for the ordering facility

```
<HTML>
<HEAD><TITLE>Joe's Shopping Service - Select Products</TITLE></HEAD>
<BODY>
<H1>Joe's !!catalog!! Catalog</H1>
<H2>List of Products - Select</H2>
<HR>
<FORM METHOD=POST ACTION="/cgi-bin/billing.pl">
<INPUT TYPE="HIDDEN" NAME="catalog" VALUE="!!catalog!!">
<H3>Please select products you would like to order</H3>
<SELECT NAME="products" SIZE=4 MULTIPLE>
!!options!!
</SELECT>
<P><INPUT TYPE="reset" VALUE="Reset">
<INPUT TYPE="submit" VALUE="Total Up Prices">
</FORM>
<BR><HR SIZE=3 WIDTH=70%><BR>
!!footer!!
</BODY>
</HTML>
```

CGI Script for the Product Selection Page

Listing 10-9 gives the CGI script we will use to fill in the product selection template. Save this CGI script as select.pl and move it to your CGI script directory. On our server, it's

```
/etc/httpd/cgi-bin/select.pl
```

Listing 10-9: select.pl, the CGI script that generates the product selection form

```
#!/usr/local/bin/perl5
# select.pl
# Displays the product selection form.
```

```perl
push(@INC, "cgi-libs");
require 'templates-lib.pl';
   # Uses FillTemplateFile($template, %var_values);
require 'forms-lib.pl';
   # Uses GetFormInput();
require 'catalog-lib.pl';
   # Uses  SetCatalog($catalog);
   #       GetProducts();
   #       GetProduct_Name($product);
require 'footer-lib.pl';
   # Uses GetFooter($template);
MAIN: {
    print "Content-type: text/html\n\n";
    # Extract information from the URL.
    local(%input) = &GetFormInput();
    local($catalog) = $input{'catalog'};
    print "<!-- Got catalog: $catalog -->\n";
    &Catalog::SetCatalog($catalog);
    local($productID) = $input{'product'};
    print "<!-- Got product ID: $productID -->\n";
    # Set template variables.
    $vars{'options'} = &getOptions($productID, $catalog);
    $vars{'catalog'} = $catalog;
    $vars{'footer'} = &Footer::GetFooter();
    # Substitute values of variables into template & print.
    print &Templates::FillTemplateFile("../templates/select.html",
    %vars);
}
# -- Internal Functions: --
# Constructs a set of options consisting of all of the products
# in the given catalog. The default element is pre-selected.
sub getOptions {
    local($defaultID, $catalog) = @_;
    local($options, $product, $ID, $name);
    local(@products) = &Catalog::GetProducts();
    foreach $product (@products) {
        $ID = $product->{'ID'};
        $name = &Catalog::GetProduct_Name($product);
```

(continued)

213

```
    if ($ID eq $defaultID) {
        $options .= "<OPTION SELECTED>$name ";
    }
    else {
        $options .= "<OPTION>$name ";
    }
}
return($options);
}
```

The Billing Form

The billing form shown in Figure 10-4 is generated by a CGI script, billing.pl, that fills in a page template, billing.html. Let's look at the template and then the CGI script.

The Template for the Billing Form Page

Listing 10-10 gives the HTML codes for the billing form template. Save this file as billing.html in your templates directory. On our UNIX server, the complete path is

```
/etc/httpd/templates/billing.html
```

There are several important things to notice about the billing.html form:

- It uses titles, headings, prompts, and buttons, to tell the user
    - What was done just now (Product Selected)
    - What they are looking at (Total Bill)
    - What they need to do (Confirm Order)
    - What will happen if they do it (Submit Order)

- It uses the SIZE attribute to limit the size of input fields, so the fields fit nicely on the page.

- It uses the MAXLENGTH value to make sure our CGI script doesn't get swamped by a nasty hacker entering an extremely long name.

- Both the items ordered and the total bill are passed on to the order processing script. HIDDEN <INPUT> form elements are used, just as they were in select.html.

214

This page template uses the following template variables:

- **!!items!!** is a list of each product selected, in alphabetical order, with prices.

- **!!total!!** is the total price for the selected products.

- **!!footer!!** is the generic page footer.

Listing 10-10: billing.html, the billing form page template

```
<HTML>
<HEAD><TITLE>Joe's Shopping Service - Total Bill</TITLE></HEAD>
<BODY><H1>Selections Made</H1>
<H2>Total Bill - Confirm Order</H2><HR>
<H3>You have selected the following products:</H3>
<P><STRONG>Product (Price)</STRONG>
<PRE>!!items!!</PRE>
<P><STRONG>Total:</STRONG> !!total!!<BR><HR><BR>
<EM>To process your order, we need the following:</EM><BR>
<FORM METHOD=POST ACTION="/cgi-bin/order.pl">
<STRONG>Full Name:</STRONG>
    <INPUT NAME="user" SIZE=30 MAXLENGTH=80><BR>
<STRONG>E-mail Address:</STRONG>
    <INPUT NAME="email" SIZE=25 MAXLENGTH=50><BR>
<INPUT TYPE="HIDDEN" NAME="items" VALUE="!!items!!">
<INPUT TYPE="HIDDEN" NAME="total" VALUE="!!total!!">
<P><INPUT TYPE="reset" VALUE="Reset">
<INPUT TYPE="submit" VALUE="Submit Order">
</FORM><BR><HR SIZE=3 WIDTH=70%><BR>
!!footer!!
</BODY>
</HTML>
```

CGI Script for the Billing Form

The billing form CGI script is shown in Listing 10-11. It retrieves the name and price of each item selected on the product selection form, adds the prices to get a total, and puts this information in the billing form page template. Save this script as billing.pl in your CGI script directory. On our server, it's

```
/etc/httpd/cgi-bin/billing.pl
```

Here are some things to note about the billing.pl CGI script:

- We had to add code to segregate the values that the user selected. The forms-lib.pl library adds a newline (\n) in between each of the selected values, so we used **split** to separate these values into a list, @names.

- When the user selects a product, the *name* of the product is passed to the CGI script, not its product ID. This is just the way SELECT elements work. Whatever appears next to the OPTION tag in a SELECT element is the value that is passed to the CGI script processing the form. Our script converts the name back into an object, using the function **&Catalog::GetProductByName**.

Listing 10-11: billing.pl, the CGI script that totals the selected products and generates the billing form

```perl
#!/usr/local/bin/perl5
# billing.pl
# Generates a billing form, given a list of selected products.
push(@INC, "cgi-libs");
require 'templates-lib.pl';
   # Uses FillTemplateFile($template, %var_values)
require 'forms-lib.pl';
   # Uses GetFormInput();
require 'catalog-lib.pl';
   # Uses GetProductByName($name);
   #      GetProduct_Name($ID);
   #      GetProduct_Price($ID);
require 'footer-lib.pl';
   # Uses GetFooter($template);
MAIN: {
   local($ID, $price);    # product ID, its price
   local($total) = 0.00;  # cost of all products
   local($product);
   # Extract information from the URL.
   local(%input) = &GetFormInput();
   # Catalog is available through a HIDDEN field.
```

```
local($catalog) = $input{'catalog'};
&Catalog::SetCatalog($catalog);
# Products are available from the SELECT element
local($names) = $input{'products'}; # products ordered
# If no products ordered, redirect to an error file.
if ($names eq '') {
    print "Location: ../responses/billing_err_no_select.html\n\n";
}
else {
  print "Content-type: text/html\n\n";
  print "<!-- Got catalog: $catalog -->\n";
  print "<!-- Got products: $names -->\n";
# For multiple values, you must split them out by newlines.
  local(@names) = split("\n", $names);
  local($items) = '';        # Holds list of products and prices
  foreach $name (@names) {
      $product = &Catalog::GetProductByName($name);
      $name = &Catalog::GetProduct_Name($product);
      $price = &Catalog::GetProduct_Price($product);
      $items .= " $name ($price)\n";
      $total += $price; # add price to total.
  }
  # Set template variables.
  $vars{'items'} = $items;
  $vars{'total'} = $total;
  $vars{'footer'} = &Footer::GetFooter();
  # Replace the template variables in the page template and print.
  print &Templates::FillTemplateFile("../templates/billing.html",
%vars);
  }
}
```

Order Processing

Order processing is done by a CGI script called order.pl, shown in
Listing 10-12. Put this one in your script directory. Our path is

```
/etc/httpd/cgi-bin/order.pl
```

Listing 10-12: order.pl, the CGI script that processes the order

```perl
#!/usr/local/bin/perl5
# order.pl
# An order form processor.
push(@INC, "cgi-libs");
require 'forms-lib.pl';
   # Uses GetFormInput();
require 'comments.pl';
   # Uses SendMessage($sender, $recipient, $msg);
# -- Global Variables --
MAIN: {
   # Make this your own e-mail address for testing purposes.
   local($orderdept) = "joe\@infowidget.com";  # receiver of orders
   # Extract information from the URL.
   local(%input) = &GetFormInput();
   local($user) = $input{'user'};
   local($email) = $input{'email'};
   # This info is available because of HIDDEN fields.
   local($items) = $input{'items'};
   local($total) = $input{'total'};
   # Do error checking on Name and E-mail fields.
   if ($user eq '') {
    print "Location:     ../responses/order_err_no_user.html\n\n";
   }
   elsif ($email eq '') {
       print "Location: ../responses/order_err_no_email.html\n\n";
   }
   else {
       print "Content-type: text/html\n\n";
       # Set the mail msg info.
       local($message) = &getOrder($user, $email, $items, $total);
       # Send the mail message, from the user.
       &SendMessage($email, $orderdept, $message);
       print "<HTML><HEAD>\n";
       print "<TITLE>Joe's Shopping Service - Order Sent</TITLE>\n";
       print "<BODY><H1>Order Sent</H1>\n";
       print "<PRE>\n";
       print $message;
       print "</PRE>\n";
```

218

```
    print "<H2>Thank You</H2>\n";
    print "</BODY></HTML>\n";
  }
}


# -- Utility Functions --
# Create and return a text version of the order.
sub getOrder {
    local($user, $email, $items, $total) = @_;
    local($message) = "
Attn: Order Processing Department
Customer: $user
E-mail:   $email
Product (Price)
------------

$items
------------

Total: $total";
    return($message);
}
```

Required Files, Scripts, and Libraries

The order.pl script sends mail to the ordering processing department using the **&SendMessage** function that we wrote as part of comments.pl. Make sure comments.pl is properly installed in your /cgi-bin directory. On our machine, the complete path is:

```
/etc/httpd/cgi-bin/comments.pl
```

You'll need to provide the response messages you want to display when users don't enter their name and e-mail address. The HTML codes for these responses are given in Listing 10-13 and Listing 10-14. Save the files as order_err_no_user.html and order_err_no_email.html and install them in your /responses directory. On our system, the complete paths to these files are

```
/etc/httpd/responses/order_err_no_user.html
/etc/httpd/responses/order_err_no_email.html
```

Listing 10-13: order_err_no_user.html, the HTML file for responding to a user that does not enter a name

```
<HTML>
<HEAD><TITLE>Order Not Processed: Missing Name</TITLE></HEAD>
<BODY>
<H1>Order Not Processed</H1>
This program cannot process your order without your name filled in.
<P>Please return to the form and fix this problem.
<P>No order was mailed.
</BODY>
</HTML>
```

Listing 10-14: order_err_no_email.html, the HTML file for responding to a user that does not enter an e-mail address

```
<HTML>
<HEAD><TITLE>Order Not Processed: Missing Address</TITLE></HEAD>
<BODY>
<H1>Order Not Processed</H1>
This program cannot process your order without your e-mail address
filled in. <P>Please return to the form and fix this problem.
<P>No order was mailed.
</BODY>
</HTML>
```

A Persistent Object Perl 5.0 Library

We have now completed most of the code for our shopping service. Before we run the service, however, we need to implement a code library that will give our shopping service access to the product information created earlier in this chapter.

Listing 10-15 gives the Perl 5.0 code for object-lib.pl, a persistent object library. This library accesses database information that resides in a set of files on your Web server machine's local file system and converts them into Perl 5 objects as they are needed.

Save this file as object-lib.pl and put it in your /cgi-libs Perl library directory. On our UNIX system, we would save the file as

```
/etc/httpd/cgi-bin/cgi-libs/object-lib.pl
```

This library provides the following functions:

- **&GetAllObjects()** returns a list of all objects.

- **&CreateObject(**$*filename***)** returns a Perl 5.0 object that provides access to the product information contained in $*filename*.

- **&GetObject(**$*ID***)** returns the Perl 5.0 object that has the ID $*ID*.

- **&CreateObject(**$*filename***)** returns a new Perl 5.0 object and associates it with the given file. The object is assigned an ID of the *filename* without the extension (by removing the last four characters).

The object-lib.pl library also supplies the following method:

- **&Get_Value(**$*object*, $*attr*, $*persist***)** returns the value of $*attr* for $*object*. If $*persist* is True, this method retrieves the value from the appropriate file as a character string and assigns it to $*attr*.

Listing 10-15: object-lib.pl, a Perl 5 persistent object library

```perl
#!/usr/local/bin/perl5
# object-lib.pl
# Allows access to object instances stored in files.
package Object;
# -- Global Variables --
$ROOT_DIR = "..";# store files relative to /cgi-bin
$OBJECT_DIR = "$ROOT_DIR/objects"; # store objects in this directory
%OBJECTS = ();     # object cache, indexed by object ID.
# -- Functions provided --
# Gets the list of all objects, either from the cache or by reading
# them in from persistent storage (files).
sub GetAllObjects {
    local($filename, $currobj, @objects);
    local(@objects) = values(%OBJECTS); # Get the full list
    if (! @objects) {
        opendir(FILES, $OBJECT_DIR);  # Else, open a directory handle
        foreach $filename (sort readdir(FILES)) { # sort file names
```

(continued)

221

```perl
        $currobj = &createObject($filename);
        push(@OBJECTS, $currobj);
      }
    }
    return(@objects);
}
# Resolves object IDs to objects using %OBJECTS.
sub GetObject {
    local($ID) = @_;
    return $OBJECTS{$ID};
}
# In addition to its persistent attributes, each object has a
# 'ID' attribute that stores the unique name of the object.
sub CreateObject {
  local($filename) = @_;
  local($object);
  substr($filename, -4) = ''; # remove ".obj" extension, 4 chars.
  $object = &GetObject($filename); # resolved the ID to an object.
  if ($object) {
     print STDERR "Skipping duplicate object: $filename\n";
     }
  else {
     $object = bless { 'ID' => $filename };
     return($object);
  }
}
# -- Methods provided --
# Gets the value of an attribute. Reads in object file when the
# first attribute is accessed. Reads in values for persistent
# attributes on demand.
sub Get_Value {
    local($object, $attr, $persist) = @_;
    local($value) = $object->{$attr};
    return $value if $value;        # If value is cached, return it.
    $object->get_attrs;             # If no value, read all attributes.
    $value = $object->{$attr};      # Now get the value again.
    if ($persist) {                 # If persistent att, read from file.
```

```perl
        $value = &readAttr($attr, $value);
    return($value);
}
# -- Utility functions --
# Reads in an entire object, an attribute at a time.
# Only handles a single persistent attribute.
sub readAllAttrs {
  local($object, $persist_attr) = @_;
    foreach $attr keys(%vars) {
        $persist = $attr if ($attr eq $persist_attr);
        $vars{$attr} = $object->Get_Value($attr, $persist);
    }
}
# Reads an attribute value from a separate attribute directory.
sub readAttr {
 local($attr, $file) = @_;
 open(FILE, "$ROOT_DIR/$attr/$file") || print STDERR "Error: Couldn't
open $ROOT_DIR/$attr/$file\n";
 local(@file) = <FILE>; # Read in entire file
 return join(' ', @file); # Separate lines by spaces
}
# -- Utility methods --
# Gets the filename from the 'ID' attribute, reads in each
# attribute line, reads in values for attributes in separate
# directories, and assigns attribute values.
sub get_attrs {
  local($object) = @_;
  local($file) = $object->{'ID'};
  open(FILE, "$OBJECTDIR/$file.obj") || print STDERR "Error: Couldn't
open $OBJECTDIR/$file.obj for reading.\n";
  while (<FILE>) {
    chop;
    ($attr, $value) = @_;
      $object->{$attr} = $value;
    }
  }
1; # always return 1 from libraries
```

Installation Overview

Table 10-3 gives an overview of the page templates, response files, CGI scripts, and code libraries required for running the shopping service. Make sure you have all of the files in the specified directories and the files are readable by your Web server daemon.

Table 10-3: Summary of Files for Shopping Service Installation		
TYPE (FORMAT) DIRECTORY	FILE	SOURCE CODE LISTING
Page Templates (HTML) /templates	store.html	Listing 10-2
	footer.html	Listing 10-4
	browse.html	Listing 10-6
	select.html	Listing 10-8
	billing.html	Listing 10-10
Response Documents (HTML) /responses	comments_confirm.html	Listing 7-2
	comments_err_no_addr.html	Listing 7-3
	order_err_no_user.html	Listing 10-13
	order_err_no_email.html	Listing 10-14
CGI Scripts (Perl) /cgi-bin	store.pl	Listing 10-3
	comments.pl	Listing 6-3
	browse.pl	Listing 10-7
	select.pl	Listing 10-9
	billing.pl	Listing 10-11
	order.pl	Listing 10-12
Code Libraries (Perl) /cgi-bin/cgi-libs	catalog-lib.pl	Listing 10-1
	templates-lib.pl	Listing 5-1
	footer-lib.pl	Listing 10-5
	forms-lib.pl	Listing 6-2
	object-lib.pl	Listing 10-15

Running the Shopping Service

You can now run the shopping service. Visit the URL for the store.pl CGI script. For example

```
http://www.yourserver.com/cgi-bin/store.pl
```

You should see a display like that shown in Figure 10-1. Try putting in new types of catalogs and new products. Have fun!

Next Step: Making Your Service Safe

Now you're ready to consider the security issues involved in having real users running your CGI programs from real machines around the Internet. Read on . . .

## Chapter 11

Safe CGI Scripting in Perl

T o turn your Web application into a real Internet service, you'll have to consider the potential security risks. Think about it for a minute — users from all over the world are going to be running programs stored on your Web server machine. What's the worst that could happen? Plenty:

- Flaws in your Web server software, CGI scripts, or configuration options could allow intruders into your host machine, or even into other machines on your local area network.

- Private information at your Web site—your company secrets, your passwords, you name it — could fall into the hands of unauthorized hackers.

- If you are accepting payment for something you're selling, outsiders could intercept credit card numbers or other payment information.

It's a fact that CGI scripts of any kind can be a serious security risk, and Perl scripts are particularly vulnerable to attack. That's because Perl source code is often easy to get, and hackers find ways to exploit security weaknesses in the code to gain illegal access to host computer systems. Fortunately, you can significantly reduce the risks by following some simple security guidelines. This chapter offers you suggestions.

Make Sure You Know Where Your Programs Are

When you write CGI scripts, use *complete directory paths* for programs that you run from your script. For example, if you want to run an external program, such as the **grep** command, you could use the Perl **exec** operator as follows:

```
exec 'grep', $pat, 'filename'
```

However, it is safer to provide the complete path to the **grep** command, like this:

```
exec "/bin/grep", $pat, 'filename'
```

When you use the PATH environment variable, make sure you include only those directories that include programs to which you want to give users access. For example, designate a directory search path such as this:

```
$ENV{'PATH'} = '/bin:/etc/httpd/cgi-bin:/etc/httpd/cgi-bin/cgi-libs';
```

This setting for PATH would only give users access to programs in /bin, /etc/httpd/cgi-bin, and /etc/httpd/cgi-bin/cgi-libs.

Note: You should *never* include the current directory, denoted by a single dot (.), in the search path.

Put all of your CGI scripts in the /cgi-bin directory or directories directly under the /cgi-bin directory, such as /cgi-bin/cgi-libs. If you are the Webmaster, set up the permissions on these directories so only you can install programs there.

Guard Against Tainted Input

Variables that are set using information from outside the program are deemed "tainted" and shouldn't be used to run programs available on your host system, including mail programs and file transfer facilities.

Turn On Taint Checking

Perl will check for tainted variables for you.

- In Perl 4, use **taintperl** in your CGI script header:

```
#!/usr/local/bin/taintperl
```

- In Perl 5.0, use the -T flag:

```
#!/usr/local/bin/perl5 -T
```

Untaint Your Tainted Variables

You can untaint a tainted variable by extracting just the information you need. To do this, use Perl's pattern matching operator:

```
m/ / or / /
```

For example, here's how to get an untainted seven-digit phone number from user input stored in *$tainted_input:*

```
$tainted_input =~ /(\d\d\d-\d\d\d\d)/;
$untainted_address = $1;
```

Now **perl** will not complain when you pass *$untainted_address* as an argument to another program, such as **mail** or **grep**.

Omit Unnecessary Command Shells When Calling External Programs

You may unintentionally create a security risk by invoking an external program using

- The **system** command
- A pipe (| **program**)
- Backquotes ('**program**')

When you use these methods to invoke an external program, the Perl interpreter actually starts up a command shell for you. Thus, tainted user input passed as arguments to this external program could allow hackers to execute unwanted commands on your host computer, using special characters that execute in the command shell environment. Such troublemakers could decide to remove all of your files, for example.

To avoid this flaw in your programs, don't call external programs using the Perl **system** operator like this:

```
system "grep $in filename";
```

Instead, pass the special characters (|-) to **open** and then **exec** the required program. For example, to run the UNIX **grep** program with a user-supplied input, *$in,* do the following:

```
open (IN,"|-") || exec "/usr/bin/grep",$in,'filename';
while (<IN>) {
    print "$_;
}
close IN;
```

This will run **grep** directly — without starting up an extra command shell.

You will also want to substitute for any pipe (|) commands. For example, instead of the piped **open** in Chapter 6:

```
open(MAIL, "|$MAILER -f$sender");
```

you can substitute

```
open (MAIL,"|-") || exec $MAILER,"-f",$sender;
```

Using the **exec** operator in this fashion will run *$MAILER* and provide it with input via the MAIL filehandle without starting an extra command shell.

Don't Depend on Form-Based Interfaces as Protection for CGI Scripts

Anyone sufficiently savvy can run your CGI program using a CGI URL instead of using the form-based user interface that you supply. Users can easily change values of HIDDEN fields, add more information than can normally be input into your form's text fields, and so forth. Protect your CGI script, not your form.

Control Your Server-Side Includes

Server-side includes (SSIs), discussed in Chapter 5, are a big security risk. SSIs allow users without special privileges to run CGI scripts, opening the possibility of unsuspecting users running unsafe scripts, making your host subject to intrusion. If you don't need the convenience of server-side includes, turn the includes off.

Your Web server software may allow server-side includes to be turned on only for specific users. Examine your Web server documentation or check with your Webmaster. If you can, restrict SSIs to only trusted users.

Note: If you are running on NCSA HTTPd, you can turn off server-side includes by making sure this line is in your access.conf configuration file:

```
Options IncludesNoExec
```

Protect Your CGI Scripts with Passwords

You may want to let only certain privileged users run your CGI scripts. You can use the Basic Authentication scheme to password-protect your scripts. Keep in mind, however, that because the user's name and password are minimally encrypted, they could be intercepted by anyone with enough smarts and malicious intent.

More sophisticated methods, such as public key encryption (explained just below), are necessary to guarantee the authenticity of a user.

Encrypt Sensitive Information

The most popular method of encrypting sensitive data before transmitting it over the Internet is *public key encryption.*

With this technique, everyone has *two* unique passwords: a public key and a private key. If you want to send a private message to someone, you first get their public key. You encrypt your message using this public key and then transmit the resulting scrambled message to the target user (in e-mail, for instance). They decrypt the message using their private key. No one in between you and the target user can decode the scrambled message, so the information is safe. Users who share public keys become a trusted group that can freely send private messages back and forth to one another.

PGP Encryption

PGP (Pretty Good Privacy) is a popular and free public key encryption program. PGP has been used for protecting data files, e-mail, and Web traffic. You can download the official release of PGP 2.6 from

```
ftp://net-dist.mit.edu/pub/PGP
```

See *PGP: Pretty Good Privacy* from O'Reilly & Associates (1994) or Paul Zimmerman's *The Official PGP User's Guide* from MIT Press (1995) for more information. Also, check out the Usenet newsgroup

```
alt.security.pgp
```

Read Up on Security and Consult the Experts

Information about safe CGI scripting can be found at the Web addresses listing in Table 11-1. Check with the individual authors about their materials as needed.

Table 11-1: Web Resources for Help with CGI Security

URLNOTE:	AUTHOR AND DESCRIPTION
`http://www.cerf.net/ ~paulp/cgi-security`	Paul Phillips; an overview for beginners
`http://www.csclub.uwaterloo.ca/ u/mlvanbie/cgisec`	Michael Van Biesbrouck; an intermediate tutorial; mostly Perl
`http://www.genome.wi.mit.edu/ WWW/faqs/www-security-faq.html`	Lincoln Stein; covers a range of Web security topics, including safe CGI scripting in Perl
`http://hoohoo.ncsa.uiuc.edu/ cgi/security.html`	NCSA; secure scripting tips for NCSA HTTPd

Ultimately, every data link between your CGI program and your users is a security risk; this includes your server machine, your Web server software, and all Internet hosts between you and your clients. Check out these books on Internet security:

- *Internet Security Handbook* by William Stallings (Mecklermedia Corporation and IDG Books Worldwide, Inc., 1995)
- *Introduction to Internet Security: From Basics to Beyond* by Garry S. Howard (Prima On-line, 1995)

To *really* protect your Web site and your customer's information, you can hire a security expert from a company such as Bellcore:

```
http://www.bellcore.com/SECURITY
```

or IBM:

```
http://www.zurich.ibm.com/Technology/Security
```

Both companies have experience at all levels of Internet hardware and software security.

If you follow the precautions in this chapter, your Internet Service Provider will be much more comfortable about letting you run your CGI/Perl applications on its Internet host.

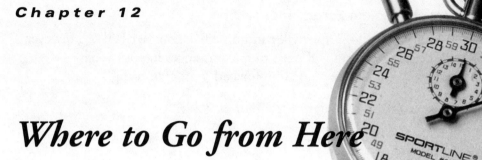

Chapter 12

Where to Go from Here

I f you use the Web on a regular basis, you know that Web tools and technology are changing every day. It's important to be looking out for future developments so you can anticipate how your way of working might change.

In this chapter we look at where Perl and CGI are headed. We will also examine alternative ways of creating Web applications, including writing CGI programs in other scripting languages, using Web server APIs, and programming in Java. We'll wrap up with a brief discussion about accessing databases and adding a payment scheme. Finally, we'll tell you how to launch your completed Web application or service.

The Future of Perl

As we went to press, Perl 5 was still in its third beta release, 5.003. Following are locations of the latest information and developments about the evolving Perl language.

235

Updating Perl 4 Scripts for Perl 5

In general, Perl 4 scripts will run immediately under Perl 5. However, in special cases, you will need to make changes in your version 4 scripts. Follow these guidelines for Perl 5 programming.

1. Escape your at signs (@). For example, use

   ```
   mail("joe\@infowidgets.com")
   ```

   instead of

   ```
   mail("joe@infowidgets.com")
   ```

2. Put parentheses around your arguments to avoid precedence problems. Here are some examples.

   - Use

   ```
   open(SRC) || die
   ```

   instead of

   ```
   open SRC || die.
   ```

   - And use

   ```
   shift(@x) + 10
   ```

   instead of

   ```
   shift @x + 10
   ```

   - And use

   ```
   $val = scalar keys(%var) + 10
   ```

   instead of

   ```
   $val = scalar keys %var + 10
   ```

3. Use this construction:

   ```
   save::file
   ```

   instead of

   ```
   save'file
   ```

4. Use an ampersand to call a function and quotes to get a string value. For example, use

```
&form
```

for a function call instead of

```
form
```

And use

```
'form'
```

for a string value instead of

```
form
```

Here are some things Perl 5.0 won't let you do that Perl 4 allowed:

- Assign a value past the end of a string using **substr**
- Assign to read-only variables, such as *$1*

For more details, consult the Perl 5 documentation.

Note: According to Larry Wall, creator of Perl, I/O-intensive Perl 5 code should run about as fast as the same code in Perl 4. Compute-intensive operations are about 25% faster in Perl 5.

Perl 5 Platform Availability

Perl 5 is available for most UNIX, Windows, and Macintosh platforms. To find out if Perl 5 has been ported to your platform, see the Perl 5 Porters Page:

```
http://www.hut.fi/~jhi/perl5-porters.html
```

If you have a problem getting Perl 5 running on your machine, first check the searchable list of bug reports at

```
http://www.perl.com/perl/bugs
```

If you can't find a fix for your problem, post a detailed description to the Usenet newsgroup

```
comp.lang.perl.misc
```

Locating Perl 5 Code Libraries

Perl 5 is an object-oriented language that strongly encourages reuse through shared class libraries. Perl 5 class libraries are being developed for these and many other tasks:

- Profiling, benchmarking, and tracing
- Access to FTP and SMTP
- Object-oriented GUI programming in Tk and X/Motif
- Encryption and authentication using PGP, DES, MD5, and Kerberos
- Creating and processing forms and dynamic Web pages
- Creating and processing HTTP messages

Expect to see quite a few new and exciting Perl 5 modules coming out soon. For example, you'll find one called Penguin at

```
http://coriolan.amicus.com/penguin.html
```

that can speed up your coding of Internet commerce and mobile agent applications.

Perl 5 modules are not shipped with the Perl 5 release—they must be downloaded separately. To find out the status of a Perl 5.0 class library or extension, check the newsgroup

```
comp.lang.perl.modules
```

or visit the Perl 5 module list on the Web maintained by Time Bruce:

```
http://www.metronet.com/perlinfo/modules/00modlist.long.html
```

You can also look in the CPAN code archives mentioned in Chapter 13, Useful Resources.

Limitations of Perl 5

Although Perl 5 is a powerful language, some modern language features are missing from its implementation.

No Compiler

Perl 5 was designed to be both a compiled and interpreted language, but so far no one has completed a compiler for it.

No Multithreading

Because multithreading is absent, you can't write programs that run independently in parallel within Perl itself. Of course, if your operating system supports multithreading, you can run multiple independent Perl programs that way.

The Bottom Line

It is well worth the effort to learn Perl 5 and upgrade your earlier-version scripts. You will be able to easily integrate object classes from Perl contributors across the world.

More Information on Perl 5

For more information on Perl 5, look for the updated Perl books from O'Reilly & Associates. Also, look at the Perl 5 page at

```
http://www.metronet.com/perlinfo/perl5.html
```

or browse the manual at

```
http://www.metronet.com/perlinfo/perl5/manual/perl.html
```

Using Other CGI Scripting Languages

Here are a number of other popular scripting languages used for CGI programs.

- **Python** is an interpreted language written by Guido van Rossum. For more information, see the Python page at

```
http://www.python.com
```

- **REXX** is another interpreted language first seen on IBM systems, now popular for CGI programming. See the REXX home page at

```
http://rexx.hursley.ibm.com/rexx/
```

- **Tcl** is an embedded command language written by John Ousterhout. It is popular because of its simple graphics extensions called Tk. In addition, however, Tcl has recently gained popularity as a CGI programming language. See the Tcl Web page at

```
http://www.sun.com/tkl
```

The Tcl code library called **SNTL** provides routines to handle CGI forms and output HTML pages.

- **Visual Basic Script:** Microsoft has mdoified their popular Visual Basic language for use on the Internet. For the latest, see

```
http://www.microsoft.com/intdev/vbs/vbs.html
```

The Bottom Line on Other Languages

To date, Perl is the scripting language of choice on the Internet. Perl has significant momentum, a wide base of users, cross-platform availability, and an international software archive (see Chapter 13 for details).

More Information on Other Scripting Languages

For more information on scripting languages for CGI/1.1, check out the newsgroup

```
comp.lang.misc
```

The Future of CGI

CGI was originally developed for the NCSA HTTPd server and was subsequently implemented by other Web server manufacturers, including Netscape Communications Corporation. In this section, we look at where the Common Gateway Interface might be going, both on and off the standards track.

Windows CGI/1.3

Robert Denny has proposed CGI extensions for Windows 95 and Windows NT; O'Reilly & Associates has implemented these extensions on its WebSite 1.1 Web server. For a draft specification of CGI/1.3, see

```
http://website.ora.com/wsdocs/32demo/windows-cgi.html
```

This version of CGI is suited to writing programs in Delphi Object Pascal and Visual Basic on the Windows platform. It is unlikely to become a standard because of its platform specificity, but it is an improvement over CGI/1.1.

UnCGI

UnCGI is a package written by Steve Grimm at Hyperion that processes form data before it ever gets to your CGI program or script. Each form field is turned into an environment variable, freeing you from decoding URLs as our forms-lib.pl Perl library does. You can use UnCGI with Perl scripts on UNIX platforms. See

```
http://www.hyperion.com/~koreth/uncgi.html
```

Though this package is an interesting alternative to CGI, and quite useful for shell scripts and C programs, UnCGI is unlikely to become a standard because it only works on the UNIX platform. It is not supported by any major commercial vendors.

An IETF CGI Standard

David Robinson put CGI on the standards track by drafting a proposal to the Internet Engineering Task Force in October 1995. His draft can be found at the following official FTP site:

```
ftp://ds.internic.net/internet-drafts/draft-robinson-
www-interface-00.txt
```

The Bottom Line on Standards

NCSA probably will not establish a version of CGI newer than CGI/1.1, since they no longer control the Web server market. It is possible, however, that smaller Web server manufacturers will band together to push the IETF standard forward.

Web server manufacturers such as Microsoft, Netscape, and Spyglass may push CGI forward—especially on the Windows NT platform. Because Web server manufacturers want to capture market share, it's more likely that each company will try to enhance its own server APIs (see the upcoming discussion), instead of proposing new CGI extensions. We'll have to wait and see what develops.

More Information on the CGI Standard

Watch the Web consortium pages at

```
http://www.w3.org/pub/WWW/CGI/
```

and the CGI pages at NCSA

```
http://hoohoo.ncsa.uiuc.edu/cgi/
```

Using Web Server APIs

This section discusses an alternative to using the Common Gateway Interface: developing your program using a Web server API. Such APIs can make your Web applications run faster, and they may integrate more tightly with the Web server software package than is possible through CGI. On the other hand, they are specific to the server manufacturer, thus reducing the portability of your application across Web servers and hardware platforms.

Using a Web server API, your application is compiled and called directly by the Web server software. Let's take a look at the leading Web server APIs.

Netscape's NSAPI

Netscape Server API (NSAPI) works with all Netscape Web servers running on Windows NT and UNIX. It allows you to customize the way Netscape servers handle access logging, user authorization, and error handling. See the Netscape documentation, or visit

```
http://www.netscape.com/comprod/server_central/config/nsapi.html
```

Microsoft's ISAPI

Internet Server API (ISAPI) works with the Microsoft Internet Server running on Windows NT. Microsoft is shipping this Web server and API with Windows NT. Documentation can be found in the Microsoft BackOffice Developer's Kit. Or visit

```
http://www.microsoft.com/intdev/server/ISAPIAPP.HTM
```

Spyglass ADI

Spyglass Application Development Interface works with the Spyglass Server running on Windows NT and UNIX. It supports plug-in security modules for various types of authentication. For details, see

```
http://www.spyglass.com
```

GNN GNNServer API

GNN provides an embedded Tcl API and a C API for the GNNServer Web server package. For documentation, see

```
http://naviserver.navisoft.com/docs20/cgi-ch.htm
```

The Bottom Line on Server APIs

Generally speaking, programs written with a Web server API are 10%–25% faster than the corresponding CGI version. If you are writing a critical application (your Web site's secure credit card transaction processor, for instance) look into porting your Perl code to C or C++ and hooking it into a Web server through the vendor's API. Otherwise, stick with CGI and Perl; that combination is more flexible and is portable across Web servers and hardware platforms.

More Information about Web Server APIs

To learn about Web server APIs, see each individual Web server vendor. A comprehensive and up-to-date list of Web servers and their features can be found at

```
http://www.webcompare.com
```

Using Java

The Java programming language from Sun Microsystems is a portable, multithreaded, object-oriented language that allows for execution on the client machine instead of the server machine. This gets you fast, local execution of code, enabling dynamic animations and games over the Web. It's a big contrast to CGI programming, where most computation takes place on the server machine.

Netscape is now supporting JavaScript, a scripting language version of Java that will process HTML forms and other operations previously handled by CGI programs. Before jumping on the Java bandwagon, however, you should give some consideration to the implications of client-side execution.

Security Considerations

No matter how secure the Java developers have made the Java interpreter, local administrators and individual users will be nervous about external Java programs running amok on their local machines. It's possible that these external programs may disable key features your program needs—or bring Java down altogether.

Java programs running on Netscape browsers cannot access the local file system. This restriction seriously limits the kinds of programs you can run over the Web using Java—at least on the Netscape Navigator browser.

Several known security flaws in Java have alarmed corporate administrators, because these flaws would allow external users to access sensitive corporate data.

Performance Considerations

Java programs may actually be slower than the corresponding CGI program. If a Java program requires access to centralized data, that data must be downloaded to each client machine. A considerable performance hit may result—especially if the client machine is much less powerful than the server machine and frequently accesses centralized information.

Integration Considerations

For pattern matching and file processing, accessing external programs and databases, and running operating system calls, Perl is a superior language. These are precisely the kinds of operations that you want to execute when running a Web-based service that handles payment, transactions, and information access.

The Bottom Line for Java

It is likely that Java programming and CGI programming will peacefully coexist. For example, there's no reason why you can't write a GUI using Java that runs on a client machine and communicates with a Perl 5/CGI program running on a server. We recommend that you learn both languages. Then decide on the functions you want to run on the client side and which ones you want to run on the server side.

Learning More about Java

Over the next year, more Java books than you can count will be published. The *60 Minute Guide to Java,* another book in this IDG Books Worldwide, Inc. series, is a good start. Another good one is *Hooked on Java* (Addison-Wesley, 1996) by Arthur van Hoff, Sami Shaio, and Orca Starbuck. Also, look for the official Java series from Addison-Wesley, written by the Java development team.

Accessing Databases

This book has described CGI programs that access files to create dynamic Web pages. You can significantly extend the power of your CGI programs by accessing a database and using this structured data to create your dynamic Web pages. Let's review some of the Perl packages now available for accessing databases.

DBPerl

DBPerl is a public-domain package from Harris, Inc., that provides SQL (Structured Query Language) access to relational databases via special HTML codes. For details, see

```
http://www.harris.com/DBperl/
```

Sybperl

Sybperl, created by Michael Peppler, lets you access Sybase databases and works with Perl 5. See

```
http://www.sybase.com/WWW/Sybperl/
```

Oracle World-Wide Developer's Kit

You can access Oracle databases from your Perl CGI programs using the Oracle World-Wide Developer's Kit. It's free, available from Oracle at

```
http://dozer.us.oracle.comn:8080/
```

The package includes ORAYWWW, a public-domain program that can generate tables and HTML forms from Oracle 7 databases. ORAYWWW was built with OraPerl, which can be found on the

```
comp.sources.misc
```

newsgroup.

The Perl 5 Generic Data Base Interface (DBI)

Perl 5 also provides a generic database interface called DBI. You can use DBI to access Oracle, Ingres, Informix, Msql, and DB2 databases. Check out the CPAN archives in Chapter 13, Useful Resources, for details.

The Bottom Line for Database Access

Database integration will very likely become a part of most Web server software packages in the future. For now, it's getting easier to integrate CGI programs and databases using public-domain and commercial software. My recommendation is to find out what database facilities you have available at your site and what integration options your Web server software provides. Then, if your Web server software doesn't offer what you need, examine the CGI facilities mentioned in this section.

More on Database Access from Web Applications

IDG Book's *Foundations of World-Wide Web Programming with HTML and CGI* (1996) provides details on how to set up a gateway to a database using CGI and Perl. Several Web server books also include information on database access, so check your local bookstore.

Providing a Payment Method

In this section, we discuss methods of providing a secure payment method for your Web services. You now have a number of options for accepting payment from customers without divulging their private information: First Virtual Accounts; credit cards; and the digital cash system. Let's look at each of these options.

First Virtual Accounts

You can register your Web service with First Virtual Holdings, Inc. Your users give First Virtual a credit card number and contact information, and in return they receive an account number. Your CGI scripts use this account number for billing.

You'll need special software. For details, see

```
http://www.fv.com
```

or send mail to

```
info@fv.com
```

The book *Digital Cash: Commerce on the Net* by Peter Wayner (Academic Press, 1996) includes First Virtual software and explains how First Virtual accounts work.

Credit Cards

If you run your CGI scripts on secure Web server software, then you may opt to transmit and receive credit card numbers over the Web. The browser encrypts the data and the server decrypts it for your scripts—all transparently.

SSL (Secure Sockets Layer) is the most accepted method for secure transmission, of sensitive information over the Internet. For an explanation of SSL, see

```
http://www.netscape.com/info/security-doc.html
```

MasterCard and VISA have agreed on Secure Electronic Commerce (SEC) as a standard for credit card transactions on the Web. For up-to-date information, see MasterCard's Web site:

```
http://www.mastercard.com
```

> **Caution:** Although secure payment schemes can prevent credit-card number piracy as a number flows across the Internet, these options can't protect an individual's desktop. A devious hacker can always look over your shoulder as you type, plant a virus in a CGI script, or install a Trojan horse in your Web browser that captures a credit card number as it is input.

Digital Cash

Digital cash is a debit system as opposed to a credit system. Web users purchase digital "E-cash" from a real bank. As users buy goods and services on the Web, special software subtracts the purchase amount from their account at the bank. Digital cash is suitable for smaller purchases and is totally anonymous—neither the bank nor the merchant knows the items purchased, and the merchant doesn't know the identity of the customer. For more information, visit

```
http://www.digicash.com
```

The Bottom Line on Payment Methods

Numerous Web server manufacturers are building secure payment schemes into their servers. These will work with popular Web browsers, but it's doubtful that any single payment scheme will become standard on the Internet. Instead, cybershop owners will have to accept multiple methods of payment to remain competitive.

More Information about Payment Methods

See the book *Internet Commerce* by Andrew Dahl and Leslie Lesnick (New Riders Publishing, 1996) for more information about these and other Web payment options.

Announcing Your Service to the World

Once your application or service is ready for the big time, you will want to advertise it on the Web. There are a number of available services for registering new Web offerings.

Yahoo!

Yahoo!, Inc., will list your application's or service's URL for free. Visit

```
http://www.yahoo.com
```

and select Add URL. Yahoo! also sells advertising options for launching your new Web service with a bang.

The NCSA What's New Page

NCSA's What's New Page also lists new Web sites. To add your URL to their list, visit

```
http://www.gnn.com/wn/whats-new-form.html
```

New Web advertising services are becoming available every month, so check *Internet World* magazine for the latest and greatest services. In general, you get what you pay for.

And Away You Go . . .

Now you're all set to begin your journey into providing services on the Web. Before you move on, have a look at the resources in the next chapter, so you can learn more about CGI and Perl.

Chapter 13

Useful Resources

This is an introductory book, so you'll surely outgrow it in time. Here in this chapter you'll find a list of places to look for more information as you work toward gaining skill with Perl and CGI.

Perl Books

In addition to the Perl books listed in Chapter 3, you might want to look at the following books:

- *The Perl 5 Desktop Reference* by Johan Vromans (O'Reilly and Associates, 1996) is a handy quick reference guide for Perl 5.0.
- *Perl 5 Interactive* by John Orwant (Waite Group Press, 1996) includes programming tips for using Perl 5.0.
- *Software Engineering with Perl* by Carl Dichter and Mark Pease (Prentice Hall, 1995) includes a disk with lots of useful Perl 4 scripts and techniques for doing rapid prototyping.
- *Teach Yourself Perl 5 in 21 Days* by Dave Till (Sams Publishing, 1996) covers Perl 5 in detail.

Perl Resources on the Web

To keep up with the latest developments in the Perl language, check out the following Web sites.

www.perl.com

The Perl Language home page at

```
http://www.perl.com/perl
```

is the definitive Web resource for Perl information, maintained by Tom Christiansen. It contains hyperlinks to software, documentation, bug reports, and numerous on-line resources. You can also get details on corporate support packages and training available from The Perl Consulting Group.

MetroNet

```
http://www.metronet.com/perlinfo
```

The latest news on Perl 5.

Nexor

```
http://www.nexor.co.uk/public/perl/perl.html
```

Documentation, archives, and Perl software.

Northwestern University

```
http://www.eecs.nwu.edu/perl/perl.html
```

Perl reference materials and hyperlinks.

Yahoo!

Some general Perl hyperlinks are listed on Yahoo! at

```
http://www.yahoo.com/Computers/Languages/Perl/
```

There is also an assorted list of Web-related Perl hyperlinks at

```
http://www.yahoo.com/Computers/World_Wide_Web/Programming/Perl_Scripts/
```

CPAN FTP Sites for Downloading Perl Code

Most Perl code can be downloaded from CPAN (Comprehensive Perl Archive Network) FTP sites around the globe.

- In the U.S.:

```
ftp://ftp.delphi.com/pub/mirrors/packages/perl/CPAN
```

- Outside the U.S.:

```
ftp://ftp.funet.fi/pub/languages/perl/CPAN/README.html
```

The main site on FUNET is in Europe; Delphi is a mirror in Massachusetts. There is probably a mirror site near you; check FUNET for a complete listing of member sites.

CGI Programming Books

The following books provide more information about CGI scripting, including examples in Perl.

Overview and Introductory Books

- *Foundations of World-Wide Web Programming in HTML and CGI* by Ed Tittel, Mark Gaither, Sebastian Hassinger, and Mike Erwin (IDG Books Worldwide, Inc., 1996). Gives details on how to access databases and other topics not covered in this book. Includes a CD-ROM.

- *HTML and CGI Unleashed* by John December and Mark Ginsburgh (Sams.net Publishing, 1995). Covers HTML and CGI scripting and offers some short Perl examples.

- *Introduction to CGI/Perl: Getting Started With Web Scripts* by Steve Brenner and Edwin Aoki (M&T Books, 1996). Offers a basic introduction to HTML forms and CGI forms processing.

Programming Books and Advanced Topics

- *Web Programming Secrets with HTML, CGI, and Perl* by Ed Tittel, Sebastian Hassinger, and Mike Erwin (IDG Books, 1996). Contains a variety of Web programming tips and Perl programming tools.

- *The Webmaster's Guide to HTML: For Advanced Web Developers* by Nathan J. Miller (McGraw Hill, 1996). Useful CGI programming tips and examples.

- *How to Set Up and Maintain a World-Wide Web Site* by Lincoln Stein (Addison-Wesley, 1996). A complete guide for Webmasters; includes lots of useful CGI scripts in Perl 4.

- *Build a Web Site* by net.Gensis and Devra Hall (Prima Publishing, 1995). Includes a chapter of annotated CGI program examples in Perl 4.

CGI/Perl Code Libraries

Besides the ones in this book, a number of other Perl CGI libraries are available.

cgi-lib.pl

By Steven Brenner; public-domain code for form processing; Perl 4.

```
http://www.bio.cam.ac.uk/cgi-lib/
```

CGI.pm

By Lincoln Stein; public-domain code for creating and processing forms; Perl 5.

```
http://www-genome.wi.mit.edu/ftp/distribution/software/WWW/
```

net.Form

By net.Gensis; generates forms and provides database integration.

```
http://www.netgen.com
```

CGI/Perl Program Archives

The following program archives contain a large number of Perl CGIs that you might find useful.

- *CPAN* has a large CGI script area.

```
ftp://ftp.funet.fi/pub/languages/perl/CPAN/scripts/
```

- *The NCSA Script Library* is one of the older Perl CGI archives.

```
ftp://ftp.ncsa.uiuc.edu/Web/httpd/Unix/ncsa_httpd/cgi/
```

- *The Web Developer's Virtual Library* lists CGI resources of all types and allows you to post your own information.

```
http://www.stars.com/Vlib/Providers/CGI.html
```

- *The CGI Source Code Index for Perl* from LPAGE Internet Services lists some Perl scripts you might find useful.

```
http://www.Lpage.com/tindex/Perl_Scripts/
```

- The *WebTools* page sponsored by NetForce Development, Inc. includes the ever-popular Counter 4.0 Perl script.

```
http://www.webtools.org
```

CGI/Perl Newsgroups

The Usenet newsgroup comp.lang.perl has been supplanted by these three newsgroups:

- *comp.lang.perl.announce*—Announcements about the Perl language
- *comp.lang.perl.misc*— Programming issues and bug reports
- *comp.lang.perl.modules*—Discussion group for people programming Perl 5.0 modules

  In addition, the newsgroup

```
comp.infosystems.www.authoring.cgi
```

is devoted to CGI programming issues, mostly in Perl.

CGI/Perl Mailing List

If you are developing your own Perl 5 CGI modules, you may want to join the CGI-Perl mailing list. Send an e-mail message containing the word 'info' on a line by itself to

```
cgi-perl-request@webstorm.com
```

A searchable archive of this mailing list is available at

```
http://www.rosat.mpe-garching.mpg.de/mailing-lists/CGI-Perl/
```

The modules referred to on this list can be found at

```
http://www-genome.wi.mit.edu/WWW/tools/scripting/CGIperl/
```

This mailing list is mostly for people developing Perl 5 modules, but you can find out a lot about how these modules work by searching the mailing list archives.

CGI/Perl Programming Tips for Your Platform

Tips for programming Perl CGI scripting are available for three popular platforms: UNIX, Windows NT, and the Macintosh.

UNIX

These Web sites include up-to-date tips about CGI scripting in Perl, especially on UNIX platforms.

- *Clever.net* is a consulting firm with CGI experience. Visit

```
http://clever.net/self/faq/cgi.html
```

- *www.perl.com* has an expert section you'll want to check out. Try

```
http://wwww.perl.com/perl/everything_to_know/
```

- *LPAGE Internet Services* offers classes in CGI programming. See CGI tutorial at

```
http://www.lpage.com/cgi/
```

Windows NT

The Windoze Perl FAQ provides information on using Perl on Windows platforms, particularly Windows NT:

```
http://www.perl.hip.com
```

You can also join the ntperl@mail.hip.com mailing list. Send a one-line subscribe message to

```
Majordomo@mail.hip.com
```

A software library for Perl running on Windows NT is also available at

```
http://website.ora.com/software/
```

Mac

Tips for using Perl with MacHTTP and StarNine's WebStar server software are available at

```
http://arpp1.carleton.ca
```

You're On Your Way!

Congratulations. You've learned a great deal about CGI programming in Perl. You're ready to start writing those killer apps that will make the Web a better place to work, shop, learn, and have fun. Good luck—millions of Internet users across the world are counting on you.

Appendix

CGI Environment Variables and Headers

his appendix lists normal CGI environment variables, HTTP_ environment variables, and CGI headers.

CGI Environment Variables

AUTH_TYPE

Definition	The name of the scheme used for authenticating the user's identity.
Format	The only defined value is Basic, which refers to the Basic User Authentication Scheme in HTTP/1.0. This encrypts and passes the user name and password with each HTTP request.
Example	Basic

CONTENT_LENGTH

Definition	The number of bytes in the data that was submitted along with a PUT or POST request.
Format	Integer
Example	If the input is "name=Rob", then CONTENT_LENGTH is 8.

CONTENT_TYPE

Definition	The MIME Content-Type for the data submitted with the POST or PUT request.
Format	*type/subtype; param1; param2;...; paramN*
Example	application/x-www-form-urlencoded

259

Appendix

GATEWAY_INTERFACE

Definition	The version of the CGI specification with which this server complies.
Format	CGI/*version*
Example	CGI/1.1

PATH_INFO

Definition	The extra part of the path in the URL.
Format	Any string
Example	If the URL is *http://www.idgbooks.com/cgi-bin/test-cgi/debug*, then PATH_INFO is /debug.

PATH_TRANSLATED

Definition	The physical path in the file system for the URL in PATH_INFO.
Format	*/dir1/dir2/..../file*
Example	If the URL is *http://www.idgbooks.com/cgi-bin/test-cgi/home.html*, a possible PATH_TRANSLATED variable is /usr/local/etc/httpd/htdocs/home.html.

QUERY_STRING

Definition	The search part of the URL. Set by GET requests.
Format	URL encoded
Example	name=John+Smith&address=Smith%40idgbooks.com

REMOTE_ADDR

Definition	The IP address of the host making the request.
Format	IP address format
Example	128.6.4.2

REMOTE_HOST

Definition	The name of the host making the request.
Format	DNS entry format
Example	aramis.rutgers.edu (the DNS entry for the IP address 128.6.4.2)

REMOTE_IDENT

Definition	The name of the user as provided by an IDENT server running at user's site.
Format	An Internet mail address
Example	farrell@aol.com

REMOTE_USER

Definition	The login name of the user, if provided during the authentication process.
Format	A string
Example	farrell

SCRIPT_NAME

Definition	Name of the CGI script that is running.
Format	*path/program*
Example	If the URL is *http://www.idgbooks.com/cgi-bin/test-cgi*, then SCRIPT_NAME is /cgi-bin/test-cgi.

SERVER_NAME

Definition	Contains the name of the server machine that is calling your CGI program.
Format	DNS entry or IP address format
Example	www.idgbooks.com

SERVER_PORT

Definition	Contains the port number on which the HTTP server is listening.
Format	Internet port numbers
Example	80 or 8001 are common.

SERVER_PROTOCOL

Definition	Name and version number of the Web protocol used in this HTTP request. The protocol name is for our purposes.
Format	*protocol/version*
Example	HTTP/0.9 or HTTP/1.0

SERVER_SOFTWARE

Definition	Name and version of the server software.
Format	*name/version*
Example	NCSA HTTPd/1.4.1

HTTP_ Environment Variables

The following HTTP_ headers are potentially available to CGI programs. These are derived directly from request message headers.

HTTP_ ENVIRONMENT VARIABLE	DESCRIPTION
HTTP_ACCEPT	Acceptable MIME content types
HTTP_ACCEPT_CHARSET	Character sets that the client will accept
HTTP_ACCEPT_ENCODING	A list of compression schemes acceptable to the client
HTTP_ACCEPT_LANGUAGE	A list of natural languages that the client will accept
HTTP_AUTHORIZATION	User name and password
HTTP_FROM	User's e-mail address
HTTP_IF_MODIFIED_SINCE	Server returns the resource only if it has been modified since this date
HTTP_PRAGMA	A value of "no-cache" means return the uncached version
HTTP_REFERER	The resource that linked to the current resource
HTTP_USER_AGENT	The client program making the request (e.g. Mozilla)

CGI Headers

Following are all of the CGI headers that can be returned by a CGI program, with definitions, formats, and examples.

CONTENT-TYPE

Definition	The MIME type of the document you are returning to the client.
Format	Content-type: *type/subtype; param1; param2;...;paramN*
Example	Content-Type: text/html

LOCATION

Definition	Redirects the client to a given URL (Format1) or specifies that the server should retrieve and return a file to the client (Format2).
Format1	Location: *URL*
Example	Location: http://www.idgbooks.com/home.html
Format2	Location: */dir1/dir2/..../file?searchpart*
Example2	Location: /home.html

STATUS

Definition	Allows your CGI program to send a status code back to the client.
Format	Status: *Code Reason* The status codes you can return are exactly those that the server can return, as specified in the HTTP specification.
Example	Status: 401 Unauthorized

Index

H

Harvest search engine, 155–156
headers, 262
home pages, 7
host.html page template,
    112–113
hot lists, 12
<HR> element, 202
HTML (HyperText Markup
    Language), 17–18, 98
html file extension, 195
HTML/2.0-compliant Web
    browser, 87
HTTP (HyperText Transfer
    Protocol), 14
  advantages, 30
  CGI programs executable by
    daemon, 96
  environment variables, 261–262
  extensibility, 30
  header information, 39–41
  operation of, 30
  simplicity, 30
  stateless, 185
  transmitting data over Web,
    29–30
  universality, 30
  versions, 29
HTTP_ACCEPT environment
    variable, 41
HTTP_ACCEPT_LANGUAGE
    environment variable, 41
HTTP_FROM environment
    variable, 40, 131
HTTP_REFERRER
    environment variable, 40
HTTP_USER_AGENT
    environment variable, 40
hyperlinks, 4, 9, 29
hypermedia, 9

I

IETF CGI standard, 241
if statement, 63–64
@INC array, 203
#include SSI command, 106
Indeo (Video for Windows), 8
index document, 9
index operator, 65
index.html document, 9
indexer-lib.pl listing, 170–172
informative responses to CGI
    scripts, 141–147

%input associative array,
    130–131
<INPUT> element, 120–121,
    140
  CHECKED attribute, 137
  HIDDEN attribute, 211
  MAXLENGTH attribute, 121
  NAME attribute, 121, 136–137
  SIZE attribute, 121
  TYPE attribute, 121–122,
    136–137
  VALUE attribute, 122, 137
installing CGI programs, 94–96
instances, 78
Internal Server Error (500)
    status message, 144
Internet
  domain name, 14
  gateway programs, 23–24
  searching services, 11
InterNIC, 14
IP (Internet Protocol) address, 15
IPP (Internet Presence Provider),
    14
ISAPI (Internet Server API), 242
<ISINDEX> tag, 162–163

J

Java, 8, 44, 243–245
JavaScript, 244
join operator, 71
JPEG (Joint Photographic
    Experts Group), 7

K

keywords, 154
Krol, Ed, 157

L

length operator, 65
lib file extension, 77
libraries, 77–78
local operator, 75
local variables, 75
Location headers, 43–44,
    141–147
Loukides, Mike, 51
lowercase (lc) operator, 59
LYCOS, 159

M

MacHTTP, 22
Macintosh
  Perl, 51
  programming support for
CGI (Common Gateway
    Interface), 27
MacMosaic, 10
MacPerl, 51
MacWeb for the Macintosh, 10
MAIL filehandle, 132
markup language, 17
match /pattern/ operator, 65–67
match multiple occurrences (*)
    special character, 68
menus, 136–139
METHOD attribute case
    sensitivity, 127
methods, 79–80
Metronet, 50
Microsoft Internet Explorer, 10
Microsoft Internet Information
    Server (IIS), 21, 27
MIME (Multipurpose Internet
    Mail Extensions), 41–43
missing Perl script header, 92
MIT Student Information
    Processing Board, 15
modularizing programs, 73–77
Mosaic, 9, 29
Moved Permanently (301)
    status message, 144
Moved Temporarily (302) status
    message, 144
MPEG (Motion Pictures Expert
    Group), 8
multimedia information, 7
multiple-selection option menus,
    138–139

N

NAME attributes, 125
name=value pairs, 126
NaviServer, 22, 27, 29
NaviServer API, 243
NCSA (National Center for
    Supercomputing
    Applications), 9
NCSA HTTPd, 27, 29, 87
NCSA HTTPd for UNIX, 20
NCSA Web server, 105
NCSA What's New Page, 249
net.Formlibrary, 254
Netscape Navigator, 10, 18, 27,
    29, 87